PERGAMON INTERNATIONAL LIBRARY
of Science, Technology, Engineering and Social Studies

The 1000-volume original paperback library in aid of education, industrial training and the enjoyment of leisure

Publisher: Robert Maxwell, M.C.

Systems Psychology In The Schools
(PGPS-141)

THE PERGAMON TEXTBOOK INSPECTION COPY SERVICE

An inspection copy of any book published in the Pergamon International Library will gladly be sent to academic staff without obligation for their consideration for course adoption or recommendation. Copies may be retained for a period of 60 days from receipt and returned if not suitable. When a particular title is adopted or recommended for adoption for class use and the recommendation results in a sale of 12 or more copies the inspection copy may be retained with our compliments. The Publishers will be pleased to receive suggestions for revised editions and new titles to be published in this important international Library.

Pergamon Titles of Related Interest

Cartledge/Milburn TEACHING SOCIAL SKILLS TO CHILDREN:
Innovative Approaches, Second Edition

Conoley/Conoley SCHOOL CONSULTATION:
A Guide to Practice and Training

Eisenson LANGUAGE AND SPEECH DISORDERS
IN CHILDREN

Kirby/Grimley UNDERSTANDING AND TREATING ATTENTION
DEFICIT DISORDER

Morris/Blatt SPECIAL EDUCATION: Research and Trends

Wielkiewicz BEHAVIOR MANAGEMENT IN THE SCHOOLS

Related Journals
(Free sample copies available upon request)

JOURNAL OF CHILD PSYCHOLOGY AND PSYCHIATRY

JOURNAL OF SCHOOL PSYCHOLOGY

PERGAMON GENERAL PSYCHOLOGY SERIES
EDITORS
Arnold P. Goldstein, Syracuse University
Leonard Krasner, SUNY at Stony Brook

Systems Psychology In The Schools

Jeanne M. Plas
*George Peabody College
of Vanderbilt University*

PERGAMON PRESS
New York • Oxford • Beijing • Frankfurt
São Paulo • Sydney • Tokyo • Toronto

Pergamon Press Offices:

U.S.A.	Pergamon Press, Maxwell House, Fairview Park, Elmsford, New York 10523, U.S.A.
U.K.	Pergamon Press, Headington Hill Hall, Oxford OX3 0BW, England
PEOPLE'S REPUBLIC OF CHINA	Pergamon Press, Qianmen Hotel, Beijing, People's Republic of China
FEDERAL REPUBLIC OF GERMANY	Pergamon Press, Hammerweg 6, D-6242 Kronberg, Federal Republic of Germany
BRAZIL	Pergamon Editora, Rua Eça de Queiros, 346, CEP 04011, São Paulo, Brazil
AUSTRALIA	Pergamon Press (Aust.) Pty., P.O. Box 544, Potts Point, NSW 2011, Australia
JAPAN	Pergamon Press, 8th Floor, Matsuoka Central Building, 1-7-1 Nishishinjuku, Shinjuku-ku, Tokyo 160, Japan
CANADA	Pergamon Press Canada, Suite 104, 150 Consumers Road, Willowdale, Ontario M2J 1P9, Canada

Copyright © 1986 Pergamon Books, Inc.

All rights reserved. No part of this publication may be reproduced, stored in a retrieval system or transmitted in any form or by any means: electronic, electrostatic, magnetic tape, mechanical, photocopying, recording or otherwise, without permission in writing from the publishers.

First printing 1986

Library of Congress Cataloging in Publication Data

Plas, Jeanne M.
  Systems psychology in the schools.

  (Pergamon general psychology series ; 141)
  Includes index.
  1. Personnel services in education. 2. Community psychology. I. Title. II. Series. [DNLM: 1. Psychology, Social. 2. Schools. HM 251 P715s]
  LB1027.5.P585 1986   371.4   86-5095
  ISBN 0-08-033144-0
  ISBN 0-08-033143-2 (pbk.)

Printed in the United States of America

To Ruby M. Saks—
the things she stands for and
those like her I have known.

CONTENTS

Foreword ix
Preface xiii
Acknowledgments xix

PART 1 FUNDAMENTALS: THE PHILOSOPHY AND THEORY

Chapter

1. Introduction 3
2. Systems Thinking in Sciences Other Than Psychology 9
3. Transactions: Systems Thinking in Psychology's Past 18
4. Community Psychology from a Systems Point of View 25
5. Families: Good Beginnings and Good Examples 33
6. Systemic Fundamentals: A List 49

PART 2 THE MOVE INTO THE SCHOOLS

7. Systemic Issues in the Schools 85
8. School-Based Systemic Methodology 102
9. A Case Simulation 120
10. Other Approaches to Systems Psychology in the Schools 136
11. The Past and the Future 145

References 151
Author Index 157
Subject Index 159
About the Author 161

FOREWORD

Since at least the 1960s, practitioner psychologists working in community settings, such as schools, hospitals, and mental health centers, have been concerned with system change. It is no great secret that those with problems do not have these problems in isolation from other people and from their environments. We have long recognized the influence of parents on children and, more recently, have come to understand how schools, neighborhoods, friends, regional differences, and whole cultures affect the behaviors, feelings, attitudes, and values of those we attempt to help. We try to take this broader understanding of system influence into account when we conduct assessments or intervene in some way in the lives of others. Knowledge of a system in which an individual lives helps sensitize us to the problems presented for our consideration. But, for the most part, what we actually do with or for others is not always greatly changed by such knowledge. And those of us who are keenly aware that the system itself may need changing before we can do very much to help those within it are not often asked to change the system. Unfortunately, even if we are asked, we hardly know what to do to bring change about through the methods and techniques that are part of the psychological practitioner's repertoire.

Systems-oriented practitioners are faced with the dilemma of knowing that what they know is important but not knowing how to use that knowledge to actually resolve the person's problem. They know that people are parts of systems and interrelated with them in important ways. They are less certain about how to use such knowledge in ways that truly make for changes both in the person and in the setting in which that person must function.

If you are among those bothered by this dilemma, read on. Jeanne Plas has something to tell you that could change the way you think and work. Be prepared to be puzzled, upset, enlightened, and informed. Stay with the book until the end. Do not give up because the ideas presented are too foreign. If possible, arrange to have someone else read the book with you. Ideally, the book should be read as part of a graduate seminar or a professional in-service or continuing education course; but it can profitably be read alone. If you read it alone, plan to talk to yourself about it. However you do it, read it from cover to cover. You will not be sorry. You may not agree with all you read; you may be especially uncomfortable with her description of school-based intervention. You will have questions about ethics, procedures, and are likely to feel that there is too much to absorb, much less use in any immediately practical way. But, if you let it, this book can be an important experience in your professional life, bringing perspective to your work and changing what you do from now on.

Jeanne Plas synthesizes a literature that is not usually part of the background and education of practitioner psychologists, making it applicable to a particular setting: the public school. She reviews and analyzes philosophy and theory from many fields leading to the conclusion that all things are connected and that reality is between the knower and that which is known. She asks us to set aside our established ways of viewing psychological practice, at least as we read her book, and to reconsider how we come to know; how human knowledge occurs. She connects us with Eastern philosophy and points out how much we are influenced by the Western philosophies and developments leading to logical positivism, raising questions about where that has led us and what it has kept us from knowing. She relates school psychology practice to recent developments in physics, family therapy, and community psychology through the interconnectedness of systemic thinking. If you think all this sounds esoteric, remote, and unrelated to daily practice in psychology, you are wrong. It is practical in the best sense of the meaning of the term. You can use it; if not immediately as a new way of practice, then over time as a new way of thinking and acting.

Do you believe that language has precise meaning? Can you talk professionally without using the verb forms to be and to know? Do you believe that deduction and induction are the sine qua non of reasoning and logical thought? Can you accept and then ignore a referral issue and still be deeply involved in the resolution of the referral problem? Would you agree that consensual validation is the only possible form of validation? If you want change to occur, does that change have to be the goal of your intervention? Do you believe in cause and effect? Which is more important in professional practice, things or ideas? Do you think that science and practice can be value free? Which of these persons have influenced your thinking: Lightfoot, Polonyi, Lewin, Dewey, Barker, Bateson, Selvini-Palozzoli, Capra, Maturana, Adelbert Ames, Bentley? Are these questions important? You bet they are! They are at the very center of our professional behavior. This book will introduce you to ideas and people who may not have been part of your education or, perhaps, known to you only in a peripheral way. If you have become interested in family systems therapy, some of these ideas and names may be familiar. I doubt, though, that they have ever been brought together as Jeanne Plas has done in this book, and I am reasonably certain that no one else so far has attempted to make *systemic* thinking (as contrasted with systems approaches) applicable to school psychology practice.

Schools and families are, in my view, the major important factors in our lives. We have begun to understand how members of families interact and talk to one another and how these interactions and communications can be understood and those involved helped to change the ways they relate to one another. We have less understanding of the connectedness of language, rules, and behaviors of those who live and work in schools.

There is a resurgence of interest in how school psychology can best serve schools and schooling, wherever it may occur. More than a few scholars are breaking new ground and providing the field with creative ideas about its potentials, bringing to the field ideas from many specialties in psychology and from other disciplines. It is an exciting time for school psychology, perhaps a "make or break" time, during which it can prove itself useful or else give way to those who can.

Jeanne Plas tells us that a new world view of human conduct is emerging and that it is time to consider how this view applies to schools. She also explains that it will not be easy to accept this view; that "new ground does not get broken without much sweat and aggravation." She encourages us to try, to learn, and to enjoy. It is especially important to note that enjoyment is part of what she asks us to consider; that our work and our struggle to understand what really happens in classrooms and in school buildings can be done with good humor, the excitement of discovery, and the headiness of seeing our world through new eyes.

So, read, struggle, learn, and enjoy!

Jack I. Bardon
Excellence Foundation Professor
of Education and Psychology
University of North Carolina

PREFACE

In 1976, at Peabody College of Vanderbilt University, I began teaching a doctoral seminar that presented the philosophical and theoretical foundations of the psychology department's combined program in clinical, community, counseling, and school psychology. A few years earlier, this systems-oriented doctoral training program, labelled Transactional-Ecological Psychology, was one of the first in the country to gain American Psychological Association accreditation in the new combined category (cf., Plas & Dokecki, 1982). The goal of the program was to educate scientist-professional psychologists who would work in one (or more) of the major professional practice settings. Further, the program sought to offer its students a specific frame of reference within which to think about the scientific and professional issues they would encounter as students and, later, as employed psychologists. The perspective was transactional and ecological. A somewhat different description of this perspective could be gained depending upon which faculty member or senior student was asked. That is still pretty much the case within the program. The lack of a unified "party line" probably has been at least partially responsible for some of the intellectual vibrancy within the program at Peabody-Vanderbilt during the past 10 years. Such speculation aside, however, the point I need to make here is that daughter of Aristotle and Newton that I was (and still am?), I found myself faced with an over-enrolled seminar of about 24 bright, assertive doctoral students who wanted to learn about this new world view called *transactionalism*. So did I. About a week before the course was to start, it occurred to me that, for about a year, I had been missing the point in some important ways as I considered the John Dewey and Arthur Bentley (1949) version of transactional thinking, which was to be the core of the course. While modestly threatening, the situation was also fortuitous since it provided the opportunity to engage in genuine seminar-type exchange, as well as the development of out-of-class study groups, reminiscent of the early Kurt Lewin variety. And so it has gone for the past 10 years. I learn, unlearn, relearn, then start all over again with a new group of students and a new crop of books and articles. Happily, in some ways, the students have become more sophisticated with respect to systems thinking over the years (or, do

I get better at listening?). Also happily, the pertinent literature has increased geometrically both in quantity and quality over the past decade.

Always, the goal of the course has been to understand the ramifications of a nontraditional epistemology, which holds that the only phenomena to be known are those arising from the transaction between a knower and that which is to be known. Dewey and Bentley believed that human language represented that transaction. Language does not represent the thing named in any objective sense; rather, language represents a transaction between the limitations of the human's cultural background and hereditary "equipment" and whatever is "out there," available for knowing.

An important 1977–1978 study group concluded that causality, linearity and other such precious notions needed radical renovation if the integrity of the basic epistemological concept was to be preserved and pushed toward a useful model of scientific and/or professional practice. Something else thought in those days was that the major breakthrough we sought would probably occur within the scientific realm rather than the professional realm. It was obvious in the mid-1970s that the literature contained provocative theory and philosophy concerning these matters but little-or-no application either in applied or scientific psychology. We were right about the causality, linearity, etc. part and dead wrong about the scientific applications. A few people produced some interesting attempts at scientific transactional methodology (e.g., Gibbs , 1979), but there were no firecracker explosions of scientific insight.

Then, one afternoon in late 1979, one of our many perceptive graduate students, Andy Bernstein, stopped me in the hall and emphatically announced that "it" had been found—the answer to our philosophical prayers. He mentioned the words *counterparadox* and *Italy* a lot and said that he would bring around a book the next day. I really had little idea what he was trying to tell me, so I remained unconcerned when he did not show up with the book for a week or so.

Selvini-Palazzoli and her colleagues (1978) had produced a work that described a new approach to intervention with families in "schizophrenic transaction." Reading it was one of those rare and memorable experiences in which a book, picked up almost casually, is still in your hands hours later as you juggle other responsibilities in order to finish-the-thing-no-matter-what before you go to bed that night. The first couple of chapters focus on the theory supporting an innovative approach to family therapy with previously "incurable" families. The rest of the volume intersperses the theory among detailed descriptions of the techniques derived from it.

My intellectual life took a turn after that—as has the thinking of many who have consulted that work and the allied thinking of intellectual giants such as Gregory Bateson and Humberto Maturana. Time has been spent learning to understand the basics and forging meaningful syntheses of ideas from systems thinkers of similar persuasion across a variety of sciences and applied professions. And always (always!) this process involved the use of my very Aristotelian, very Newtonian (very Western) mind. The square peg in the round hole analogy may be trite, but it is oh-so-apt in this particular case. Dragging a 20th century linear mind into systemic theory is not easy. That is part of the reason why it has been important to me to produce in this book as understandable a version of this systemic "reality" as I possibly could. I hope I have succeeded. Depending upon the level of systems sophistication and the degree of commitment to Western realities, some persons probably will find the treatment of the major ideas full of redundancy while others may find the issues in need of further explanation. Wherever one falls on this continuum, I hope that in reading this book some new ideas will be encountered and some enjoyable moments will be had.

The purpose of the book is twofold: To present a synthesis of ideas that bear on systems thinking and systems practice in psychology, and to develop a model for the application of a specific type, systemic psychology, in the public schools. Systems psychology is a subdiscipline that has been around for quite some time. Most of the work has been theoretical; some has been empirical; not nearly enough has been applied. A system is defined here as an organized set of relations that compose an organic whole. Those psychologists oriented toward systems are concerned with the relations within and among groups. They are interested in the structures and processes that create systems and make them "work." Rather than focusing on the individual, systems psychologists let the system stand as the unit of study or the unit of intervention. A variety of systems approaches are available in and out of psychology today. While there are sometimes vast differences among them, it is arguably accurate to say that all human systems psychologists reject the idea that an individual develops attitudes and behaviors in isolation; rather, the system is seen to influence (or control) such human activities. Within the myriad of available approaches to thinking about and working with organic systems, that called *systemic* is of special interest here. Systemic psychology represents a remarkably different way of thinking about the world. An appreciation of its major ideas often results in a radical shift in one's understanding of reality as well as one's orientation toward the practice of psychology.

Since its origination, the work of this particular brand of systems psychology has remained largely within family therapy circles, where it has created a revolution of sorts. At the very least, the systemic orientation required family therapists to redefine some of their basic beliefs. Many of those who work within this model report impressive changes in family dynamics over a relatively short period of time. Those are pretty dramatic claims — especially in the absence of extensive empirical evaluation. Nonetheless, the systemic version of psychological practice has not only held its ground, it has captured the imaginations of more and more practitioners each year, usually with the same outcome—satisfaction with the results.

It is time that systemic methods get a thorough evaluation within the public schools. Many believe that the schools are the best proving-ground for most innovative psychological approaches. Others worry that the public school setting provides nothing but a trial by fire. They believe that the nature of that system almost precludes success, especially with innovative techniques. Precisely because the schools compose one of America's most complex systems, it makes sense to me that important systems-oriented approaches must necessarily be evaluated there. Perhaps the schools have proven such a problem for psychologists precisely because traditionally they attempted to apply individually oriented methods in a setting that is importantly influenced by groups and systems. The schools tried to take strategies that work in a clinic or private therapy office and make them successful within a context that is not organizationally capable of responding to the needs of so many individual students as well as the needs of overworked and, thus, unfocused support personnel and teachers.

Systemic psychology is one of the most promising systems approaches available today. It also seems to be one of the best suited for the public schools. This book provides rationale for each of these claims. The core of the volume is concerned with presentation of basic systemic ideas and the elaboration of a model for systemic practice in the schools.

The book is divided into two parts: The first provides an introduction to systems philosophy and theory, with emphasis on systemic thinking. The second section presents theory and method for a systemic approach to intervention in the schools.

Part 1 contains six chapters. Chapter One presents an introduction to systems theory through comment on the relationship of philosophy and science and the characteristics of Eastern and Western world views. Chapter Two illustrates examples of systems thinking in sciences other than psychology; the work of Gregory Bateson, Fritjof Capra, and Humberto Maturana is emphasized. Chapter Three concentrates on the history of systems thinking in psychology's past. Gestalt psychology, transactional functionalism, and field theory are connected to the pioneering work of John Dewey and Arthur Bentley.

Chapter Four discusses examples of systems work in community psychology. The pioneering theory and research of Roger Barker on behavior settings are connected to comments concerning "sense of community" and values in public policy. Chapter Five presents a description of systemic approaches to family therapy. The methods of the Milan Associates and the work of Lynn Hoffman, Brad Keeney, and Peggy Papp form the essence of the chapter. Chapter Six provides a list of fundamental systemic perspectives. Each is explained in detail and practical methods are suggested for developing these specific ways of thinking.

Part 2 contains five chapters that focus on systems psychology applied to the school setting. Chapter Seven presents the special issues that must be considered as systemic theory and method are exported to the schools. Chapter Eight describes systemic strategies that are particularly adaptable to the schools and provides suggestions for the establishment of the intervention team that might carry them out. Chapter Nine presents a case simulation. Highlights of the case are described from team formation through the conclusion of the intervention period.

Chapter Ten outlines representative examples of promising approaches to nonsystemic systems psychology in the schools. Each of these systems models is categorized as an ecosystem, liaison, school psychology, or systemic-related approach. Chapter Eleven provides comments on the history of the systems movement as it relates to future possibilities.

In addition to presenting in-depth consideration of a particular kind of systems psychology, the book contains certain chapters that present alternate models and others that illustrate the use of these perspectives in settings other than schools and in sciences other than psychology. Thus, the treatment of systemic psychology for the schools is placed in context; history and current connections are important.

My experience with the ideas the reader will encounter in the following chapters has been marked over the years by times of frustration, joyful insight, challenge, and hope. At the moment, I hope that the results of my work will help to limit the reader's own frustration and to increase his or her periods of insight.

ACKNOWLEDGEMENTS

Special thanks to Jack Glidewell for volunteering to read and comment on the manuscript. Thanks are due also to Jerry Frank at Pergamon for being not only helpful but pleasant. Nancy Rankin Plas merits some praise for stepping in to help when help was needed. It is necessary, also, to recognize early and important input from Augie Hermann, Larry Newton, and Mark Lewis. A good person, David Yarian, deserves much for his always-useful comments on style and substance. Most of all, indebtedness is to the well over 150 doctoral students who have passed through the TEP seminar since 1976. We spent hours and hours together, thinking about trees and Coke cans, causality and whether or not "it was really there." They were bright; they were thoughtful; they knew how to have a good time. All of that was the difference that made a difference.

PART 1

FUNDAMENTALS: PHILOSOPHY AND THEORY

During a golden age, almost everything that glitters is real gold.
— Ortega y Gasset

1
INTRODUCTION

Philosophy is not the concern of those who pass through Divinity and Greats, but of those who pass through birth and death. If the ordinary man may not discuss existence, why should he be asked to conduct it?
— G. K. Chesterton

A new set of very interesting and promising ideas has begun to find its way to the cutting edge of most major scientific disciplines and many of the humanities as well. While it may be true that there is nothing really new under the sun, it is also reasonably true that these particular ideas are at least new under the Western sun. While some of them have been around for centuries in the East, their widespread emergence in the midst of Western science during recent times has been remarkable and dramatic.

In psychology, these ideas currently are called by a variety of names. The terms *systems psychology* and *systemic psychology* are becoming somewhat conventional and are the labels most often used throughout this volume. However, various other terms seem to be sufficiently descriptive and occasionally, perhaps, more precise; therefore, the topic of what to call this new theoretical perspective receives some detailed consideration from time to time throughout the following chapters. Rather than adopting a standard linear way of looking at the thoughts and feelings of human beings and the ways they behave in groups, this newer thinking is much more concerned with *patterns* of functioning. Searching for the causes of human activity ceases to be important. Inductive and deductive logic make room for other types of rationality, such as reasoning by analogy. Understanding human language patterns is critical. Everything is viewed as dynamic rather than static. Spontaneous change can be expected under certain circumstances. Working with wholes instead of pieces of the whole is fundamental. While this list of concepts does not represent the entire set of principles that form the web of interconnecting notions supporting systems theory, they give the flavor of what the excitement is all about.

Originally in the development of psychology some of the systems-oriented ideas were of practical value in research on visual perception. Later, their applicability was tested in clinical and community psychology. Today, the subfield of family therapy has become the proving ground for some of the most exciting developments. As is the case with most revolutionary ideas, controversy and emotional response to the issues are rather common in family therapy circles. In a subsequent chapter, the issues that have grown out of research and practice in systemic family therapy will be analyzed in detail. What family therapists have already learned, as well as their puzzlements, becomes invaluable as systems ideas are carried into the practice of psychology in the schools.

While it has taken a bit longer for systems thinking to gain popularity in the education-related fields of psychology, such as school psychology, it may well be the case that some of the most notable advancements might occur in educational systems. Many of the basic concepts associated with this new way of viewing the world sometimes can be best observed and utilized within complex systems, such as families and schools.

PHILOSOPHY AND SCIENCE

Speculation on the nature of reality has been the official business of philosophers for hundreds of years and the unofficial business of most of the rest of us for thousands of years longer than that. The way things "really" are all too often seems to be a well-kept secret from the human beings who inhabit the Earth. Early on, we developed a kind of guessing game we play with the universe as we try to pry loose its secrets. We speculate that the Earth is flat; then, we begin to guess it is round. We speculate that all 2-year-olds have an inborn tendency to be terrible and that there is no fool like an old fool. We tend to think that when you're out of sight you're out of mind; we also suspect that absence makes the heart grow fonder. We guess that the universe is unfolding according to a predetermined plan but also believe that one person's free choice can change the course of history.

At the grocery store, the car wash, an airline terminal, or restaurant— or in our own kitchens—when we stop to really hear what is being said around us, we discover that much of ordinary conversation is basically philosophical. We want to know what life is all about and, since the universe does not send each of us a registered letter containing a description, we spend a lot of time speculating on the nature of the realities we live each day. Each of us is a philosopher at heart. Philosophies become culture. Multiple cultures become politics; and then we play the guessing game with an identifiable opponent and much more than a game seems to be at stake.

When we look at the beginnings of recorded history we discover that much of what we have found can be thought of as philosophical speculation—in ancient Greece with Socrates, Plato, Aristotle and their predecessors, in early Eastern cultures through Lao Tsu and Confucius, in the early Hebrew writers, and even in the hieroglyphics found on Egyptian walls. Religious leaders, royalty, and philosophers ruled the thinking world.

The systematic process of confirming hunches about reality is known as science. This specialized way of learning about our mysterious universe was a spin-off from the discipline of philosophy. In Western culture in the 17th and 18th centuries, for example, the British philosophers known as empiricists (Thomas Hobbes, John Locke, and David Hume) helped to create a climate in which science could flourish, when they speculated that what we know comes to us through our senses and that sense-related information ought to be studied carefully. Prior to this time, most philosophers believed that at least some knowledge about the world was imprinted within us at birth. Given the new mindset, disciplines such as astronomy, physics, and chemistry began to separate themselves from philosophy. The most recent discipline to form itself and to separate from the patronage of philosophy has been psychology, a science that is barely over 100 years old. In a fascinating comment on the development of science in general, Thomas Kuhn (1962) pointed out that the sciences furthest removed from human beings, such as astronomy, were the first to develop; those most intimately related to humans, biology and psychology, were the last. Regardless of the date of their births, all sciences seem to have repudiated their philosophical roots once they became established in the culture. Each sought the answers to speculative questions in the laboratory rather than in the armchair, the tavern, or the church. However, the old speculation that you can take the child out of the country but not the country out of the child seems to have special applicability here. Most scientists who trust only information that can be seen, heard, or touched in the laboratory are, nonetheless, fully faceted human beings elsewhere and find themselves as engaged in armchair philosophical speculation as any other person might be. Indeed, within the practice of the sciences themselves, there has been a recent, rather widespread rediscovery of the contributions of a philosophical mindset. An outstanding example can be found in the work of Fritjof Capra, work which will be considered in greater detail in subsequent sections of this volume. Capra, a theoretical physicist, has been making important connections between modern physics and Eastern philosophy for the past several years. The eminent natural scientist, Ilya Prigogine, is representative of an increasing number of scientists who weave references to philosophers and philosophy into their complex as well as more simplified writings. Some of Prigogine's ideas have become important stimulants for those who have been defining the practice of the kind of psychology this book is concerned with; consideration of these ideas occurs later.

Quite a bit of the thought that forms the background for this book has been borrowed from the field of philosophy or from those social and physical scientists who have rediscovered the value of adopting some of the philosopher's characteristic ways of thinking about the cosmos, while trying to unlock its secrets. This thoughtful contact with our philosophical roots has enriched some of the work found today in virtually every discipline. Those who practice psychology in the schools will find increased attention to philosophic ideas to be equally as rewarding as do those in other fields.

In recent times, those who toil in the physical sciences have been, to some extent, more enthusiastic about augmenting their work with a philosophical perspective than have social scientists. Psychology, in particular, has been somewhat reluctant to borrow not only philosophical models but also findings and perspectives from the physical sciences. As the newest science on the block and the science with the most seemingly ambiguous subject matter, psychology has felt a bit defensive to some extent, not wishing to rely on the achievements of more advanced and, thus, more respected sciences. Nor has psychology wished to be associated with the intellectual "softness" that is often — and erroneously — attributed to philosophy. Adding to the generalized discomfort with physical science approaches was an address to the American Psychological Association in 1955 by the prize-winning physicist, J. Robert Oppenheimer (1956). He cited the efforts of some mid-20th century psychologists to provide an analogy between concepts in physics and psychology. Oppenheimer spoke of the "nervousness" this caused him, saying that such analogies "have to be taken with very great caution" (p. 134) due to the apparent differences in subject matter. Historically, this invited address served to practically obliterate psychology's attention to the physical sciences for about 20 years. In academic psychology, for example, reference to the Oppenheimer address still is occasionally made today by someone arguing the merits of avoiding physics as a model for anything related to psychology. However, many have come to realize that the 1955 psychological audience simply did not have the background necessary for a clear understanding of Oppenheimer's message. A careful reading of the technical physics jargon in Oppenheimer's address is not only easier than it must have been 30 years ago, it leads to different conclusions, given the knowledge base available to today's reader. After explaining the basic differences between classical mechanics and the newer quantum mechanics, he let us know that it seemed to him that "the worst of all possible misunderstandings would be that psychology be influenced to model itself after a physics which is not there anymore, which has been quite outdated" (p. 134). Oppenheimer, and others since him, found fault with adopting analogies that focus on the contributions of Newtonian, mechanistic physics, not on those that emphasize concepts associated with discoveries at the subatomic level.

What we have come to know about matter at levels smaller than the atom has stimulated theoretical speculation, which has proven to be valuable in social science fields. The connections are provocative and exciting. Throughout this volume, these discoveries and speculations are presented, and applications in various areas of psychology are discussed. School systems are natural arenas for the application of these newer approaches to understanding human functioning. We can expect that more and more examples of this type of psychological theory and practice will begin to emerge in the schools during the closing years of this century.

WORLD VIEWS

At any given point in historical time and geographical location, a set of perspectives can be identified that is used by most people to make sense out of the world. This set of perspectives contains the prevailing philosophical speculations about the nature of humanity and the rest of the universe, is attuned to the history of human achievements relevant for the times, and is shaped by local events and structures as well. For the most part, our world view is so basic that we are rarely aware of it. Sarason (1981) has written that this characteristic viewpoint "is not motivated; it is received, imbibed, a kind of given, a basic outline within which motivation gets direction. Unlike Freud's unconscious, always striving for expression, the world view is always expressed in our language, ideas, goals, and perceptions" (p. 47).

To some extent, world views are individually idiosyncratic, depending upon the unique history we each possess. I may believe, for example, that all fathers behave in a certain way — probably because mine did. Such perspectives are also regionally idiosyncratic to some degree. For example, if you are from Missouri, you need to be shown. If you are from Texas, you think bigger is better or, at least, the world view of the rest of us suggests that you think that way. And so it goes.

Moreover, history has shown us that some perspectives are common across regional and even national boundaries, and some of these perspectives may span centuries. This kind of world view is what we are concerned with here, since the systemic thought we are talking about seems to be a part of a newer Western world view that is still in the process of emerging.

Perhaps conveniently, and probably correctly, we have in the past identified an Eastern way of thinking as opposed to a Western mode. An Eastern view includes a focus on wholes rather than parts. It views human beings as part of nature rather than as entities that are superior to nature. An Eastern mind searches for patterns when trying to understand the world. We think of the Eastern world view as having been in place since the fifth or sixth century before Christ.

Having originated with Aristotle, the Western mind set is believed to have been firmly in place in European and American countries since the sixteenth century when scientific and technological achievement began to compel Western minds. The Western mind is said to be linear; i.e., oriented toward thinking in straight lines. We are concerned with the most direct way of getting from here to there in our thinking. We reason in direct routes from the general to the particular or the other way around. Western thinking tends to be mechanistic, relying on basic billiard ball notions of cause and effect. Searching for the cause of something is a favorite pastime; so is thinking in terms of dualisms. We talk about a clean mind in a clean body, for example; the unity of our being is not a concept we refer to very frequently.

Often, we refer to this Western set of perspectives as Newtonian. Sir Isaac Newton, originator of the laws of motion fundamental to classical physics, relied on all these notions as he developed his brilliant theories concerning the operation of bodies in space.

The ideas forming in modern physics (often called quantum mechanics) are based on perspectives that clearly are not Newtonian and, thus, not classically Western. Yet, Western minds are developing these ideas in physics and they have spread to other disciplines as well. Thus, many are beginning to say that a radical shift in the Western world view has already taken place. At least, there is a tendency to believe that a new world view is developing in the West. The systems-oriented ideas contained in this book are part of this new way of trying to make sense out of the world.

2
SYSTEMS THINKING IN SCIENCES OTHER THAN PSYCHOLOGY

Without my work in Natural Science I should never have known human beings as they really are. In no other activity can one come so close to direct perception and clear thought, or realize so fully the errors of the senses, the mistakes of the intellect, the weaknesses and greatnesses of human character.

—Johann Wolfgang von Goethe

Before turning to a consideration of systems approaches to psychology in general and psychology in the schools in particular, it is important that we spend some time thinking about systems ideas as they have occurred in other sciences. Not only will this approach give a historical appreciation of the development of this kind of thinking, it also will provide an excellent introduction to the relevant concepts that are of greatest importance to those who practice this kind of psychology today.

Most of the ideas fundamental for systems thinkers originally were created in other fields. Some have come from physics and biology, while others have developed in fields such as chemistry and cybernetics. The ideas have been adapted for use in psychology, and not all systems psychologists rely on the same package of concepts. While most of the ideas are complementary, various psychological researchers and practitioners emphasize those which have seemed most useful or have demonstrated the greatest possibilities in their specific applications. Thus, each psychological systems psychologist seems to offer allegiance to an almost idiosyncratic choice of relevant physical sciences and thinkers. Such is the case with many developments of knowledge within our information-exploded Western culture. A good idea seems to take hold in a variety of places and is available for purchase or loan from each of them.

BATESON, BIOLOGY, THE FAMILY, AND STORIES

The late Gregory Bateson (1956; and Bateson, Jackson, Haley, and Weakland, 1979) was an anthropologist, biologist, occasional psychologist and sociologist, and one-time husband of Margaret Mead. Bateson was a craggy-looking senior citizen at the time of his death—with an appearance of the kind fondly associated with Einstein or even Eisenhower. Gregory looked like someone's father—as, indeed, he was. Mary Catherine, his daughter, figured prominently in his earlier writings as the child who would engage with Gregory in what he called *metalogues*. These were discussions between daughter and dad that gave us a feel for his deeply sensitive nature as well as some further information about what he was trying to explain. Gregory was a theoretician (and philosopher to boot) who could think so differently and write so obscurely that, until fairly late in his career, only reasonably courageous and wildly visionary people could boast of having read any of his works from cover to cover.

Bateson's contributions to the body of systemic thought are still being discovered. We will know much more about his offerings by the close of this decade. By that time, Batesonians will be able to understand his existing writings more fully, as well as those in the last volume of his works, which Mary Catherine is preparing for posthumous publication.

At the Palo Alto Veterans Administration during the 1950s, Bateson and others (1956) introduced the double bind theory of schizophrenia, a useful conceptualization for family therapy and one that merited him the distinction of being considered one of the founders of that therapeutic movement. Bateson reasoned that human beings react to ideas and not to things. For example, your response to a lion is a response to the idea of a lion, including its capabilities and needs, and not directly to the object itself. Ideas are the substance of communication and all messages "can be magically modified by accompanying communication" (1972, p. 230). A lion in a zoo is quite different from a lion in your driveway. Bateson reminds us that when your fingers are crossed, the meaning of your message is altered dramatically. He saw that in the schizophrenic families he worked with, the schizophrenic child was unable to respond to the crossed-finger kind of content in communication. Consider the following example:

> A young man who had fairly well recovered from an acute schizophrenic episode was visited in the hospital by his mother. He was glad to see her and impulsively put his arm around her shoulders, whereupon she stiffened. He withdrew his arm and she asked, "Don't you love me any more?" He then blushed, and she said, "Dear, you must not be so easily embarrassed and afraid of your feelings." The patient was able to stay with her only a few minutes more and following her departure he assaulted an aide and was put in the tubs. (1972, p. 217)

The child was receiving double messages but could not comment on that—an important component of healthy communication. Given the contradictory messages received, schizophrenic children in Bateson's study seemed to feel damned-if-they-did and damned-if-they-did-not. Punishment became inevitable and, rather inevitably as well, these children themselves became masters at sending double bind messages. They also became adept at discomfirming their own feelings and thoughts since double bind communication often carried that kind of message. For example, a parent in Bateson's study might have said, "You didn't really mean to say that" in response to the child's criticism of the parent. The child learned to accept the parent's version of the child's own reality.

Bateson and his coworkers thought that several components are necessary for the development of double bind patterns of family communication. Two or more persons must repeatedly engage in patterns of communication containing a primary negative injunction (such as, "Do not do that or I will punish you") and a secondary injunction conflicting with the first (such as, "Do not see this as punishment" or "Do not ever submit to this kind of directive") and a third injunction prohibiting the victim from simply pulling out of the relationship.

Bateson tells us that the double bind experience is similar to that the pupil of the Zen master encounters as the pupil is told, "If you say this stick is real, I will hit you with it. If you say this stick is not real, I will hit you with it. If you say nothing, I will hit you with it." As you find yourself blocked by that set of proscriptions, you experience what life is like in a schizophrenic household. While the Zen pupil is developing within an environment where he or she eventually learns simply to take the stick out of the master's hand, the schizophrenic child lives in a world where the only safe set of actions seems to be to respond to one of the messages, accept punishment for having failed to respond to the other, and—we are free to suppose—hope for a more successful day tomorrow.

Bateson was interested in *levels* of communication. During the transmission of any given message, information can be sent on a variety of levels. Unhealthy communication patterns contain much confusion across levels. However, the same type of communicational "confusion" is responsible for the success of humor, art, poetry, and other forms of creative communication. The double entendre, when recognized, often can create a belly laugh; the double message, when absorbed literally, can create a bellyache.

In the 1970s, Bateson turned his full attention to his primary passion, biology, as he sought to discover the relationship between human patterns of communication and the rest of nature. His lifelong love affair with living things, ranging from the crab and the daisy to the schizophrenic family, led him to a detailed and creative set of suggestions concerning the similarities shared by creatures of all kinds. His thesis was that mind and nature are twin aspects of the same phenomenon—that anatomy was a transform of grammar. In practical terms, this meant for Bateson that biological patterns and communication patterns were of the same "stuff"—and that stuff was stories. Bateson's most often-used story over the years concerned a man who wanted to understand what human thinking was all about and asked his computer one day, "Do you compute that you will ever think like a human being?" After considering the question in machine-like fashion, it printed out the words: THAT REMINDS ME OF A STORY.

Boldly, Bateson told us that

> The fact of thinking in terms of stories does not isolate human beings as something separate from the starfish and the sea anemones, the coconut palms and the primroses. Rather, if the world be connected, if I am at all fundamentally right in what I am saying, then *thinking in terms of stories* must be shared by all mind or minds, whether ours or those of redwood forests and sea anemones. (1972, p. 13)

Bateson believed that biological patterns and language patterns represented the same phenomena; he spent his last years providing descriptions of the "patterns which connect." Thus, a fundamental Batesonian idea, which is coming to have relevance and practical utility for systems psychologists, has been the need for development of processes of reasoning by analogy; i.e., reasoning in the form: "this is to this as that is to that." Bateson called this process *abduction*, in contrast to other forms of logic, such as deduction (reasoning from the whole to the part) and induction (from part to whole). Abductive reasoning looks for similarity of pattern across seemingly disparate phenomena. This is a form of reasoning that many of us employ each day as we say such things as, "That reminds me of my father"; "It's just like the old house except it's brick"; "That look on your face means storm clouds are gathering."

While Bateson did not provide a detailed set of examples of abductive reasoning in ordinary English usage, it is wise to do so as we begin to catch hold of this important concept. Consider, then, such ideas as "She did not fall too far from the tree," or, "He's a chip off the old block." Each represents the end product of abductive reasoning and means pretty much the same thing: that the child and the parent have similar behavior patterns. In our language, numerous shortcut methods are used to express the conclusions we reach subsequent to reasoning abductively. For example, when we say, "Turn the tuning knob counterclockwise," we mean that the person should turn in the opposite direction to the traditional movement of hands on a clock. We are asking our listener to reproduce a familiar pattern of movement in a totally different realm of activity. We are reasoning by analogy. Some time ago in contemporary American culture, the expression, "Where's the beef?" was borrowed from a commercial advertisement on television and used extensively in order to reproduce the same message pattern in areas of living quite removed from that of the commercial. For months (and perhaps for years to come) when a context was discovered where the main ingredient of a desired and "paid for" entity was less substantial than expected, Americans could be heard to utter the well-worn phrase. We were saying to one another, "this situation is just like the one in the TV commercial"; we were relating to patterns and applying abductive logic.

Bateson believed that this type of reasoning created the possibility for human storytelling and that it was of crucial importance for an understanding of human nature as well as the rest of nature. Looking for patterns and redundancies across the various aspects of thought and behavior is, for many, an important component of contemporary systems thinking. Bateson is to be credited with providing much of the impetus for attention to this often-used but little-studied capability of the human mind. Application of abductive reasoning is stressed throughout the discussions of systems psychology in the remainder of this book. Additional contributions of Bateson will also be cited later, as they relate to topics under discussion. His was a powerful, multidisciplinary mind, and living systems of all types seemed to totally captivate and compel him. We can expect Bateson's genius to become commonly known before the end of the century.

CAPRA AND THE OBSERVING AND OBSERVED SYSTEMS

Fritjof Capra (1975; 1982) is a rather tall Austrian who possesses somewhat piercing eyes and has an open-to-experience manner about him. He is one of those persons who seems destined always to appear to be just a bit more youthful than he is. Capra has been known to say that he discovered his vocation (physics) while teaching people how to ski in the Austrian Alps. He wrote that while watching a summer afternoon ocean he experienced the possibility that all the universe dances the Hindu dance of Shiva (1975). Wherever he may be, he probably gives the impression of a man with a mission.

His has been a consistent and powerful voice in the contemporary movement to find important similarities across philosophy and science. Trained in high energy and theoretical physics, he enjoys a reputation as the original popularizer of the notion that Eastern philosophy is impressively redundant with some of the discoveries in quantum mechanics; i.e., at the level of atomic and subatomic reality. In recent years, he turned his attention to culture and health, while explicating the redundant patterns he sees across various subject matters.

Capra's message is similar to Bateson's as he describes the patterns which connect seemingly different phenomena, such as the dance of an electron and the dance of an Eastern mystic. When speaking, he has often illustrated this point by superimposing bubble-chamber photographs of particle interactions on pictures of dancing Hindu bronze statues. The effect is dramatic — as has been the effect of his work on the development of the systems theory we are concerned with here.

Capra (1975) tells us that common themes can be traced across all Eastern religions, whether they be Hindu, Buddhist, Taoist, or Zen. One of these themes concerns the philosophical speculation that all "things" are connected; it concerns the ideas of unity and interdependence. He points out that the world experienced by subatomic physicists occasions the same ideas. Interconnectedness and unity appear as basic concepts within most models of atomic reality. Through appeal to the theoretical work of Bohr, Heisenberg, Stapp, and Bohm, Capra has presented very readable descriptions of models of phenomena at the atomic level. He illustrates interconnectedness and unity by virtue of demonstrating to the reader that nothing at that level can be studied in isolation. All reality there can only be known through a description of its *relationship* to other phenomena.

One of the most important relationships to consider involves the observer with that which is observed. Capra accepts the Heisenberg (1958) interpretation that the act of observing a subatomic phenomenon necessarily alters or contributes to the phenomenon under study. The only reality that can be known is the one that results from the unity of observer and observed. This idea is of critical importance for some systems psychologists and receives great attention in the following chapters. Due to the efforts of Capra, and others who interpret physical science ideas for use elsewhere (e.g., Guillemin, 1968; Zukav, 1979), the important idea of observer-observed unity has become available for practical use in the field of psychology. When considering that nothing can be known objectively or independently at the atomic level, Capra writes that

> The solid material objects of classical physics dissolve into patterns of probabilities, and these patterns do not represent probabilities of things, but rather probabilities of interconnections. Quantum theory forces us to see the universe not as a collection of physical objects, but rather as a complicated web of relations between the various parts of a unified whole. (1975, p. 138)

Capra reminds us that what we observe in subatomic reality are not phenomena, themselves, but rather what we presume to be the consequences of those phenomena. We cannot see nor hear an electron, for example; we can only come to know this phenomenon through the clearly identifiable bits of information that laboratory instrumentation proceeds to record during the observation process. While explicating the profound consequences for knowing which are the results of this inescapable situation, Capra joins many others (eg., Langer, 1942; Berger & Luckmann, 1967; Shands, 1971) in stressing that our language is only a language of object-experience. It is a language born of direct sensory experience. As a result, it is woefully inadequate to the task of describing what we cannot see, hear, or touch. Nonetheless, we are forced to use our thing-oriented Western linear language to describe phenomena at an atomic level and from a systems perspective. In both cases, miscommunication and misunderstanding often result. Thus, attention to reorganizing our language use is critical for the adoption of a systems approach to the practice of psychology. Fortunately, scientific theoreticians like Capra and Bateson, and other writers such as Bertrand Russell (1960), have offered some excellent suggestions, which at least point in the linguistic direction we need to go. This language theme surfaces repeatedly across disciplines and across subareas of systems-oriented psychology. Thus, major portions of the following chapters are devoted to a discussion of language usage and alternatives in systemic psychology.

Most recently, Capra has turned his attention to a systems view of life with specific focus on concepts of health. He has written that

> The systems view looks at the world in terms of relationships and integration. Systems are integrated wholes, whose properties cannot be reduced to those of smaller units. Instead of concentrating on basic building blocks or basic substances, the systems approach emphasizes basic principles of organization. Examples of systems abound in nature: cells are living systems; so are the various organs and tissues of the body, the human brain being the most complex example. But systems are not confined to individual organisms and their parts. The same aspects of wholeness are exhibited by social systems — such as an anthill, a beehive, or a human family — and by ecosystems, which consist of a variety of organisms and inanimate matter in mutual interaction. What is preserved in a wilderness area is not individual trees or organisms but the complex web of relationships between them (Capra, 1982, pp. 266–267).

Using this perspective, Capra provided several examples of a systemic approach to health. Among these has been a detailed discussion of the contrast between contemporary Western medical practice and the role of shamanism (1982). Across the ages and cultures that have incorporated shamanism, the shaman has relied on a wholistic view of health that finds symptoms to be a natural expression of a condition that belongs to the whole system. In the view of a shaman, it is not just an arm or heart that is in need of attention but the entire person and the socio-cultural context in which the person is embedded. When symptoms emerge, the shaman looks toward individual jealousies and group meanings as readily as to issues of muscular flexibility and weakness. The shaman's role has focussed on systems assessment, and one of the major interventionist functions of the shaman has been to help the individual relate his or her situation to the broader context — to help the person find meaning for the symptoms in the needs of the whole.

Capra supports the call for a return to this kind of perspective in modern healing practices (cf., Engel, 1977). The re-emergence of a consideration of the whole person-in-context during the diagnosis and healing process is an example of applied systems thinking.

It is important that a theoretical physicist such as Capra has made the journey from subatomic particle physics to the life of a tribal shaman. He invests that journey with meaning and, like Bateson, convinces us of the need to adopt a multidisciplinary approach to the issues that surround us today. The gold that we have been trying so hard to mine—across all fields of human endeavor—may turn out to be those patterns and redundancies we find emerging across disciplines and subject matters. Maybe each part is a reflection of all other parts and the whole in which it is embedded.

MATURANA, EPISTEMOLOGY, AND CHANGE

Humberto Maturana (1975; Maturana and Varela, 1980) is middle-aged, Latin American, and short. In person, he wields one of those infectious personalities that finds us wanting to romp with him through whatever deliciously absurd scene from living reality that he is depicting at the moment. Maturana is witty—with the capacity to laugh at himself as well as you and me. In addition, when speaking, he has the ability to clarify some of his complicated, Western language-encumbered ideas concerning the nature of change and how people come to know anything in the first place. It is also true that most of us find it much easier to listen to him than to read him. Trained, in part, as a psychologist, Maturana's original well-known scientific contribution dealt with the patterns of communication between the retina and the brain. His later contributions (some with Francisco Varela) have been almost exclusively in biology, with occasional identifiable forays into the philosophy of science.

Many of the terms in use in contemporary American systemic family therapy have been borrowed from Maturana's collection of frequently used concepts: terms such as perturbation, instructive interaction, recursive patterns, and autopoiesis. Thus, these specific ideas are best left for inspection within the context of the family therapy discussion that follows. Maturana's more general views concerning epistemology and change are best dealt with at this point.

Maturana, like Prigogine, adopts the view that living phenomena are capable of sudden transformation—of discontinuous leaps to another level of organization. A living system with a permeable boundary in process of rather wide oscillations (or swings, if you will) under certain circumstances can spontaneously change. This idea can be used effectively in psychology, especially within systems psychology, when it comes to be fully understood with reference to a variety of psychological subject matters. Currently, the concept of discontinuous change is one greatly relied upon in systemic family therapy practice.

Epistemology is a philosophical term referring to a set of postulates concerning the way human knowledge occurs; it refers to speculation concerning how we come to "know." There is, of course, no generally accepted epistemological point of view that is held across all philosophies and sciences. Your epistemological point of view depends upon your general philosophical and/or scientific orientation. The concept of epistemology, itself, is probably the premier concept among all those we will discuss in reference to systemic psychology. For years, conventional wisdom took it for granted that we come to know things in a rather objective way through experience with them — through our senses. Epistemological issues were pretty well confined to philosophy until discoveries in subatomic modern physics forced us to reconsider our assumptions. Since the qualities of the observer are so intimately associated with the observed at the level of subatomic reality, we were forced to enquire whether it might not be true that all reality we come to know is influenced by the biological "equipment" we bring to bear upon it. We were forced to consider the possibility that a reality independent of ourselves might not be available for inspection. We could not get *to* it (as it were) because the act of trying to know about something might always influence that something.

The kind of speculation represented in the previous paragraph is epistemological speculation; and, it is a specific kind of epistemology. It is systemic. Maturana, like all other major thinkers represented in this volume, ascribes to a systemic epistemology, which holds that the reality that we come to know is born of the inseparable relationship of the observer to the observed. He talks about the "subject dependent" nature of science, stating that any scientific position must begin with the nature of the subject (observer) as its starting point.

John Dewey and Arthur Bentley (1949) first brought this concept of observer-observed unity to the social sciences, showing that the act of naming — the act of applying language — in effect, "disturbs" the objective reality that social scientists wish to learn about. This concept is of great importance for systemic psychology and is another topic that will receive important attention later on. It is a concept that received fundamental attention from Maturana, although he has not relied on the Dewey-Bentley approach to the issue, since he operates from a position in biology rather than the social sciences.

The ideas we surveyed in this chapter, in various combinations, provoked psychologists who have a systems orientation to develop new ways of conducting psychological research and practice. We will inspect some of the best examples of this work in the next chapter.

3

TRANSACTIONS: SYSTEMS THINKING IN PSYCHOLOGY'S PAST

The world of experience belongs to the basic word I-It . . . The basic word I-You establishes the world of relation.
— Martin Buber

While systems thinking historically has been influential within many of the subdisciplines of psychology, five branches of psychology stand out as having fundamental reliance on a systems orientation. In order of development, these are Gestalt psychology, transactional functionalism, field theory, and community psychology and family therapy. The most contemporary of these, family therapy and community psychology have greatest applicability to the issues that pertain to schools and, thus, they will receive attention in the following two chapters. Mention of the Gestalt, functionalist, and field theory approaches is important, however, and presentation of these points of view will aid the discussion of family and community systems orientations which follow.

GESTALT PSYCHOLOGY

It is said that, in 1910, Max Wertheimer hastily left a train in Frankfurt, Germany, in order to purchase a toy stroboscope. He had been gripped by an exciting idea while in the midst of a vacation, which he quickly abandoned. The university at Frankfurt saw fit to allow him to begin immediate work testing his hypotheses and a couple of younger psychologists joined him in his pursuits. The eldest of the two assistants, Wolfgang Kohler, eventually became famous for research with apes in the Canary Isles and later, in 1959, was elected a president of the American Psychological Association. In Frankfurt that summer of 1910, Wertheimer, Kohler, and the youngest member of the team, Kurt Koffka, made psychological history by developing ingenious experiments showing that some visual perception activities were processed in the brain rather than at the level of the retina in the eye. They showed that the brain always tries to simplify things—it prefers to work with wholes rather than parts. The German word *gestalt* sometimes translated as "whole," came to represent this system of psychology.

Kohler's later work with apes suggested that the brain has a tendency to focus on relationships and does not attend only to objects, as some had previously assumed. Kohler's apes were observed to put sticks together in order to develop a tool long enough to topple a banana that had previously been out of reach. Gestalt psychologists thought of this as insight learning and claimed that human beings preferred this mode of cognition over trial and error learning. They asserted that people would always learn through insight rather than trial and error, when all the pieces of a puzzle were present so that *relationships* could be observed.

This reliance on attention to relationships is one of the characteristics of systems approaches. It is an idea that was carefully worked out within scientific Gestalt psychology during the first part of this century. When systems thinking is applied to schools, later in this book, we will see that attention to the relationship between Maggie and her friend Paul becomes more important than attention given to either of them separately. It is the Maggie-Paul *relationship* that emerges as important within a systems point of view.

TRANSACTIONAL FUNCTIONALISM

During the 1940s a group of American psychologists interested in visual perception became known as the transactional functionalists. The major researchers associated with this system were Adelbert Ames, Jr., Hadley Cantril, Albert Hastorf, and William Ittelson (1949 a, b, & c). John Dewey and Arthur Bentley made important philosophical and theoretical contributions. Conventionally in the history of psychology, Dewey and Bentley are not called transactional functionalists. That term has been reserved for the group of empiricists named above. However, since Dewey and Bentley are credited as pioneers of both transactionalism and functionalism, it is conceptually appropriate to consider their work in this section.

Adelbert Ames is responsible for those oddly shaped windows and rooms that we still so often see at high school science fairs. Within one of his trapezoidal rooms, objects toward the front can appear to be much smaller than objects toward the rear, which is quite the reverse of everyday experience. Imagine your astonishment at observing a woman at the rear of a room to be several feet taller than a woman who is quite close to the front. We expect objects further from us to appear to be smaller. We know they "really" are not, however; perception of size is importantly dependent upon how far away from an object we are.

One of the main points that Ames held was that perception occurs as a result of the relationship between the observing human and the observed object. The nature of the reality that we are free to observe depends very much on where we are standing when we look. Context seems to be critical. Ames and the other transactional functionalists came to believe that we can never know anything as it "really" is. Knowledge of an absolute reality is theoretically impossible. We can only know things as they are in relationship to us. Reality depends on where and when we look at this or that, and how we look becomes extremely important as well. Ames wrote, "We have believed that our knowledge discloses the innate constitution of things apart from their relationship to us. We fail to realize that we can know nothing about things beyond their significance to us" (1960, p. 4).

As an illustration of the point, consider an ordinary wooden object containing a seat, a back, four legs and two arms. Typically, we believe this to be a chair. We are capable of insisting that it *is* a chair—"really." Yet, with the appropriate instruments we would observe that is is a whirling mass of electrons surrounding billions of neutrons. In fact, it is mostly space rather than solid. Indeed, isn't that what the object is—"really"? Ames (and the other thinkers we consider in this book) believe that the reality of anything we can come to know depends fundamentally on just how we look at it. The reality is born of the transaction between the object and the observer.

While most of the work produced by the transactional functionalists concerned an understanding of visual perception, they eventually turned their attention to social perception. In a classic article, Hastorf and Cantril (1954) offered a fascinating analysis of a memorable Dartmouth-Princeton football game, which was played at Princeton just after Princeton All-American Dick Kazmaier had been pictured on the cover of *Time* magazine. One of the Dartmouth players suffered a broken leg and Kazmaier left the field with a broken nose. Hastorf and Cantril let us know that the media had a field day trying to fix the blame for what was an unusually rough and bloody game. The introduction of their research report focused on accounts of the game that ran in the university student newspapers, the *Daily Princetonian* and the *Dartmouth*. While some might say that one (or both) newspapers produced badly biased accounts of the game, Hastorf and Cantril used the occasion to conduct a study to illustrate their point that the reality of what we see depends on where we are standing (or, in this case, where we were sitting). Let's take a minute to look at this classic game through the eyes of the respective newspaper editorial writers:

> This observer has never seen quite such a disgusting exhibition of so-called "sport." Both teams were guilty but the blame must be laid primarily on Dartmouth's doorstep. Princeton, obviously the better team, had no reason to rough up Dartmouth. Looking at the situation rationally, we don't see why the Indians should make a deliberate attempt to cripple Dick Kazmaier or any other Prince-

ton player. The Dartmouth psychology, however, is not rational itself. (*Daily Princetonian*, 11/27/51, quoted in Hastorf & Cantril, 1954, p. 129)

On the same day, the following appeared in the *Dartmouth*:

> Dick Kazmaier was injured early in the game. Kazmaier was the star, an All-American. Other stars have been injured before, but Kazmaier had been built to represent a Princeton idol. When an idol is hurt there is only one recourse — the tag of dirty football. So what did the Tiger coach Charley Caldwell do? He announced to the world that the Big Green had been out to extinguish the Princeton star. His purpose was achieved.
>
> After this incident, Caldwell instilled the old see-what-they-did-go-get-them attitude into his players. His talk got results. Gene Howard and Jim Miller were both injured. Both had dropped back to pass, had passed, and were standing unprotected in the backfield. Result: one bad leg and one leg broken. (*Dartmouth*, 11/27/51, reprinted in Hastorf & Cantril, 1954, p. 129)

Hastorf and Cantril interviewed students from both schools one week after the game and showed films of the game to several student groups in December. They collected data on whether rule infractions were considered "mild" or "flagrant" and which team was judged to be at fault. To those of us who have watched sports contests of any sort it comes as no surprise that these researchers discovered that such judgments were importantly influenced by which side of the football field a fan had been sitting on or which school the fan was attending when viewing the post-game films. The researchers comment that

- It seems clear that the "game" actually was many different games and that each version of the events that transpired was just as "real" to a particular person as other versions were to other people . . .
- In brief, the data here indicate that there is no such "thing" as a "game" existing "out there" on its own which people merely "observe" . . .
- From this point of view it is inaccurate and misleading to say that different people have different "attitudes" concerning the same "thing." For the "thing" simply is *not* the same for different people whether the "thing" is a football game, a presidential candidate, Communism, or spinach. (1954, pp. 131, 133, 134)

Thus, in social judgment as in visual perception, the transactional functionalists found the concept of an absolute, independent reality to be largely a rather useless and often misleading construct.

Dewey and Bentley

John Dewey was a psychologist, philosopher, educator, and founder of the Chicago school of functionalism around the turn of the century. Eleven years his junior, Arthur Bentley "had a place at the outer edge" of one of Dewey's classes at Chicago (Ratner & Altman, 1964, p. 51). Bentley was a philosopher, economist, journalist, and Indiana apple-grower. Eventually, these two outstanding thinkers engaged in an 11-year correspondence, which culminated in 1949 in a book called *The Knowing and the Known*. As the title suggests, the work contains philosophical speculation concerning the nature of the relationship between the person who observes and that which is observed. (cf. Plas & Dokecki, 1982.) Like each writer we have considered thus far, Dewey and Bentley believed that the only reality we can perceive is that produced from the transaction between you and whatever it is that you are engaging.

Dewey and Bentley talked about the self-actional, interactional, and transactional approaches to scientific inquiry. In the *self-actional* view, things are seen to operate under their own power and according to their unchangeable natures. If a bird takes a few short steps then flies into the air, it does so because it is the nature of birds to fly and because it was exerting its power in support of its nature. According to this view, you do as you do because you choose to do so. You are solely responsible for your actions. When you act in a way that does not correspond with your nature, you commit grievous error and possibly even sin. Thus, if you, the reader, were to take a few short steps then flap your arms up off a cliff, the unfortunate and predictable consequence would result from choosing to exert your powers in service of an activity that was not in accord with your nature.

Within the *interactional* frame of scientific reference, things are seen to be balanced in causal interdependence. If a bird flies it is because the trunk of the bird, its feathers and so forth, are in good balance with respect to wind resistances and other atmospheric factors. A person, operating within this frame of reference, who observed you flapping off a cliff would conclude that the nasty experience shortly to befall you would result from a lack of balance between your characteristics and those of the medium through which you fall — in short, you are too heavy for the air to support and that is why you fall.

Dewey and Bentley presented the *transactional* view as a system of naming things so as not to separate phenomena into artificial parts. A transactional perspective holds that the only reality we can know is born of the engagement between a knower and that which is known. In science, language represents that transaction. A transactional psychologist would insist that there is not simply one "correct" description of your cliff-flying-falling escapade. It depends on who is doing the describing: a child, a scientist, someone from Western Samoa, your psychotherapist, your mother.

The purposes of inquiry are very important within transactional inquiry, and a full description does not necessarily need to contain final appeal to notions of causality. Something can be understood rather well without relying on beliefs concerning who or what caused this or that. Is it really the wind resistance-weight factors that caused your downfall and broken limbs? Or, could the "real" cause be your Uncle Milton, who always insisted that a kid could do *anything* that was desired badly enough? Or, ultimately, isn't the cause that little green pill that you popped just 20 minutes before it became so very clear that you had always been destined to soar to great heights?

Dewey and Bentley did not engage in the scientific practice of isolating causal variables. They felt that interactional science was of great value but that it could not answer all questions of interest and it often forced us, in our search for causes, to separate things into artificial parts. When we break things up into parts, causality seems to reconnect them for us. Within a transactional perspective, we might be concerned with an uncomfortable marriage, seeking to describe the rhythms of the marriage and the ways in which the pain is expressed. Within an interactional perspective, we might describe behaviors that the husband exhibits whenever he observes his wife doing this or that. We see that each time she walks out on him in the midst of heated discussion, he breaks things. Her behavior causes his response. When we view things as a whole—that is, when we try to describe a marriage rather than the contributions of a husband and a wife—a rather different description emerges. One interesting and important aspect of transactional description is that, when focusing on wholes rather than causes, it becomes almost impossible to ascribe blame. When describing a marriage, we cannot blame the wife or husband. When describing a classroom, we cannot blame the teacher or children. Wives, husbands, teachers, and children are not available for blame when a marriage or classroom is considered from a transactional perspective. These unities are left intact. When the parts of a marriage or classroom are not brought under inspection, it is much more difficult to lay the blame on an individual person. More will be made of this point in Chapter 7 and later in Part 2, when the specifics of a systems approach are applied to schools.

Transactional reality is neither subjective nor objective. In transactional science, a person's subjective world is a matter for existential or spiritual consideration; an objective reality is impossible to know. The transactional reality that *is* available for study is born of the engagement between the knower and that which is to be known. Most often—especially in science, psychotherapeutic, or educational pursuits—this engagement is represented by language. It is our naming that gives us the best information concerning our transactional reality. If we begin talking about a chair rather than subatomic particles and waves, the words reveal what reality is available for inspection at that moment. A consideration of the role of language is crucial for a systems approach and, thus, the topic will be dealt with extensively in later chapters.

FIELD THEORY

Field theory gained its name because several of its pioneers attempted to draw meaningful analogies between field theories in physics and the concepts that were developing for the social sciences. Kurt Lewin (1951; cf. Marrow, 1969; Plas, Hoover-Dempsey, & Wallston, 1985), a brilliant researcher committed to the study of social problems, was a leading developer of field theory for psychology. Lewin's roots were in Freudian psychology and his ideas were quite complementary with those of the early Gestalt thinkers. Lewin came to the United States from Germany in order to avoid persecution as a Jew in his native country. He became one of this country's best loved psychologists, famous for his passionate pursuit of knowledge, a caring and sensitive attitude toward students, and a high degree of respect for the possibilities inherent in the human personality. Lewin was both charming and intellectually provocative. He is the author of the much-quoted phrase, "There is nothing so practical as a good theory." Much of the best of his "good theory" was field-oriented.

Lewin's major interest was in the psychological field he referred to as the "life space." This now well-worn phrase was created by him to represent all of the psychological factors present for a given person at a given time. Lewin figuratively presented life spaces and used them to plot psychological movement toward those goals seen to compel action. Life spaces typically involve persons, goals, milestones, barriers, paths, and so forth. From the field theory perspective, then, a trait such as persistence is not thought to be located solely within the individual. Persistence results from the movement of a person within the life space and is as influenced by variables located outside the person as by those within the person. Thus, Lewin helped us to begin thinking in terms of a total system when attempting to understand a personal life situation.

From a consideration of Gestalt psychology, transactional functionalism, and field theory, we can move to careful inspection of the systems approach as it is found in community psychology and family therapy. These contemporary subdisciplines have provided the opportunity for systems approaches to flourish and they provide us with excellent systems models for applicability and modification in schools.

4

COMMUNITY PSYCHOLOGY FROM A SYSTEMS POINT OF VIEW

Certainly it is untrue that three is no company. Three is splendid company. But if you reject the proverb altogether; if you say that two and three are the same sort of company, then you shall have no company either of two or three; but shall be alone in a howling desert till you die.
— G. K. Chesterton

As practiced today, community psychology has its roots in the community mental health movement (Murrell, 1973). In the 1960s and 1970s, federal money became available for community programs at a time when many applied psychologists were disenchanted with conventional models of clinical psychology. Dedicated professionals concluded that individual psychotherapy was time-consuming, expensive, frustrating, and often seemed to have a very limited payoff. Too few clients were improving too little at too great a cost. Federal money made it possible to bring psychology to the community, and community mental health centers were established across the country. Once psychology entered the community, it became dramatically apparent that individuals on whom psychology's therapeutic attention had centered for 60-odd years, had been — and still were — influenced by families, organizations, communities, and other groups, both weak and strong.

In the mid-1960s, community psychology was conceived as a subdiscipline by a relatively small group of dedicated mental health psychologists, who attended an inaugural conference in Swampscott, Massachusetts. From that moment to this one, the orienting principle common to all who write about and practice community psychology is a commitment to the belief that social systems have an important influence on the behavior and quality of life of each individual person.

Beyond this premier assumption, there is often sharp disagreement among contemporary community psychologists concerning goals, methods, and meanings. For a full description of the current identity crises in community psychology, the reader is directed to discussions written by Newbrough (1977b; 1984). Those in community psychology who adopt a systems approach compatible with the focus of this book believe with Murrell that "One looks at a group of people not in terms of their individual personalities, but as units having certain positions and tasks within a network. One looks at the relationships *between* these units, rather than at each unit as an independent entity" (1973, p. 9). These theoreticians and professionals believe that constructs such as *deviance*, *personality*, and *psychopathology*, do not reside solely within the individual. Rather, the behavioral syndromes that give expression to these constructs are products of the transaction between person and social system. Any given individual is seen as a component of the system when it is useful to do so; however, the individual is not believed to be the originator or exclusive possessor of such "things" as personality and pathology.

Within community psychology, Jim Kelly (1966; 1968) has been a popularizer of the term *bad fit*, as it describes the transactions between individual and group previously thought of as personality disorders and other forms of psychopathology. Kelly holds that neither the individual's coping strategies nor the ecology can be blamed for those behavior syndromes we have traditionally labelled as *sick*. Rather, he suggests that there is an inappropriate fit between person and environment. This theme, identified in an earlier chapter, of shifting blame from a single component of a situation to the *relations* found within a system is often well-illustrated in the systems-oriented community psychology literature.

A lifetime of classic work produced by Roger Barker (1968; Barker & Wright, 1955; Barker et al., 1978) contains many examples of provocative scientific approaches that reflect this point of view. Rather than the individual, Barker found the *behavior setting* to be the fundamental unit of study for psychology. These settings contain standing patterns of behavior; that is, behavior patterns that reflect shared expectations for the times and environments in which they occur. Behavior and physical objects are intimately related to one another. Half time at a football game, Bloomingdale's Fourth of July sale, and your Aunt Minerva's traditional Christmas dinner represent examples of common behavior settings. The behavior and the objects found in these settings are in reciprocal relation. It takes no special expertise to guess which behavior setting contains stands and field, shouting and staring. While staring (perhaps at the outlandish costume Aunt Minerva wore *this* year) might be part of the Christmas dinner setting, factors such as table and chairs, and the conventional references to the quality of the meal and the overambitious amount eaten will also be present and, thus, one behavior setting becomes easily distinguishable from another.

Barker's work has found its way into the history books. His descriptions of life in midwest towns during the 1940s are quite unequalled, providing an understanding of how communities are *of* people and also shape people. In a postscript to later work, Barker presents us with one of the most deeply critical challenges for those who seek to remove such things as personality and motivation from sole possession by the individual. He wrote

> The towns I observed from the Illinois Central trains in 1940 are still there and easily recognized despite some changes: Bypasses swing the highway around most of the towns, most have a few more inhabitants, . . . and all have replaced the old technologies with 1977 developments (television antennae; single-story, flat-roofed school buildings . . .). But the changes in the towns are less dramatic than the change in my comprehension of them. In 1940 I only asked, "What do people do in these towns?" In 1977 I ask in addition, "What do these towns do to people?" . . .
>
> The development did not come quickly. It was in part a product of the psychological data we collected on what people do, minute by minute, throughout their days. The discovery that the behavior streams of Persons A and B usually change similarly when they move between Locales X and Y (later identified as behavior settings) raised a problem: To what degree are people and to what degree are locales sources of behavior attributes? Personal experience by no means pointed solely to people. I thought of how much I behaved in accordance with my own intentions and how much in accordance with the dictates of the towns and cities I inhabited. I did know that I could not have my favorite lunch in Carbondale in 1940, or even my second or third preferences; Carbondale's restaurants fed me pork chops, roast pork, or pork steak (the economy was depressed, and pork was plentiful and cheap in southern Illinois). After a week of living in a central city, I was physically exhausted by the behavior it required of me: walking great distances (a private car was impractical, taxis were uncertain, and both were too expensive), climbing (down to subways, up to elevated trains and overpasses), and standing (for traffic lights and elevators, in queue lines). I escaped with relief to the easy locomotor life my small home town allowed me. And there was the continuing concern from 1940: "If a town exercises such control over people within so small a part of its whole domain as a single highway, to what degree does it take overall charge of its inhabitants?" (Barker and Associates, 1978*)

Barker's work has not only earned the label *systems-oriented*, it also represents some of the best work in what has come to be known as *ecological psychology*. The major focus of ecological psychology has been the influence of the environment on the person and vice versa. Not all ecological psychologists are systems-oriented — strange as that may seem at first consideration. To the extent that a person adopts an interactional frame of reference in the Dewey-Bentley sense, that person is not influenced heavily by systems thinking. Thus, if things are seen as balanced in causal inter-

---

*Note. From *Habitats, Environments, and Human Behavior* (pp. 285-286) by R. G. Barker and Associates, 1978, San Francisco: Jossey-Bass. Copyright 1982 by Jossey-Bass Publishers. Reprinted with permission.

dependence, then an interactional view is controlling observation. Many ecological psychologists are of this persuasion. They think in terms of causal sequences, in which the environment influences the individual who in turn may affect the environment. It is not the relationship between the teacher and student that is the object of attention for these researchers and practitioners; rather, the focus shifts from teacher to student and back again. This is an important distinction. It is entirely possible to be an ecological psychologist who is not systems oriented. The systemic ecologist always focuses on relations and wholes.

Barker is a good example of an ecological psychologist who thinks systemically. His concept of behavior setting represents the kind of person-environment relationship that systems-oriented thinkers believe to be a useful focus of inquiry. As defined by Barker, there are objects, persons, and processes (containing culture, expectations and so forth) in each behavior setting. Instead of concentrating on Aunt Minerva, the cramped dining room, or the Christmas goose, we look at the whole. It is the behavior setting, Aunt Minerva's Christmas dinner, that we seek to understand. From this perspective, it becomes impossible to blame anyone in particular for the lumpy gravy or the tense moments in the conversation. The limits and opportunities in the environment, the national and family culture, the number of participants, and other salient variables form a whole when the pot is stirred — and this whole is different from the simple *sum* of the parts. Furthermore, the systems thinkers tell us that such unities are well worth studying. It is not that the interactional frame of reference yields incorrect or meaningless information; rather, a focus on relationship, on system, provides us with different kinds of information. Such a focus broadens our understanding of the issues at hand.

A SENSE OF COMMUNITY

While the field of community psychology, for the most part, has not been systematic in, nor fully conscious of, its adoption of systems-based concepts, good examples of what we are talking about here can be found within community literature and models of practice. One such example is in the concept of "sense of community." Over the past 15 years, the sense of community concept has come of age. In the first major work devoted to the topic, Sarason (1974) noted that while a definition seemed elusive, "you know when you have it and when you don't" (p. 157). Recently, *The Journal of Community Psychology* (Newbrough & Chavis, 1986a; 1986b) devoted two issues to a consideration of the concept of sense of community, a concept some believe to be at the heart of what community psychology as a professional discipline is all about (Sarason, 1974, 1986). The articles in these special journal issues reveal a struggle with definition and application that is common to those who consider things from a systems perspective. Given the current constraints of most modern languages, it is not particularly easy to capture a phenomenon that represents a transaction among the histories, expectations,and environments of human beings. It is not as easy to define a relationship as it is an object; and definition of relationships forms the essence of systemic theory, no matter the discipline in which the theory occurs.

McMillan and Chavis (1986) and Chavis, Hogge, McMillan, and Wandersman (1986) work with a definition of sense of community that focuses on membership, influence, integration and need fulfillment, and shared emotional connection. In a manner reminiscent of the Barker work with the concept of behavior setting, McMillan and Chavis have presented a definition of sense of community with clear reference to culture, expectations, and environmental phenomena. For example, when discussing the contribution of membership to a sense of community, they note that boundaries are important shared symbols of membership. For example, clothing can constitute such a membership boundary when it serves as an obvious signal. Consider the Scottish kilt, the Japanese kimono, and that American classic, the three-piece grey flannel suit.

Raeburn (1986) reported on an intriguing community intervention in New Zealand, involving the establishment of comprehensive community projects and community houses. The development of a sense of community in areas where isolation and social unrest had been identified constituted the major goal of Raeburn intervention strategies, which centered around the establishment of neighbourhood houses in which community programs could be planned and established by local residents. Thus, we see that the relationship growing out of the union of specific cultural processes and physical surroundings — the sense of community specific to this setting and occasion — could become an object of intervention. Raeburn tells us that those in the local police force commented that a district in which one of the community houses had been located contained one of the lowest juvenile crime rates subsequent to establishment of the house and programs. Prior to this time, the district had contained one of the highest juvenile crime rates in the area in which these police officers worked.

COMMUNITY AND RETARDED CITIZENS

Stucky and Newbrough (1983) borrow the Barker construct of behavior setting in order to introduce their systems-related model for enhancing the relationship between communities and retarded citizens. They see the behavior setting as the "stuff" of which communities are made.

Traditionally, there has been an effort to normalize retarded persons so that they can better function within the community. Helping to make retarded persons as "normal" as possible was a major goal for early mental health workers. Such a mindset is still common today (cf. Stucky & Newbrough, 1981). Many mental health workers are greatly concerned with helping retarded persons learn new skills, social and technical, so that the communities in which they live can more easily value and accommodate them. This approach contains the implicit assumption that something is not quite right with the retarded person. The community norms are assumed to be appropriate and the normal functioning of the retarded person is assumed to be inappropriate or substandard.

Using the behavior setting concept, Stucky and Newbrough help us to shift the blame for failure away from the individual. They point out that "If normalization can be understood as a process whereby retarded persons and the community become integrated into each other, then it can be useful to speak of the creation of normal settings rather than of normal or normative people" (1983, p. 22). These writers call for community implementation of the liaison role (Dokecki, 1977; Williams, 1977). Liaison specialists can facilitate the incorporation of the retarded citizen into the life of the community. They assist the development of the community as behavior settings experience the arrival of new persons such as those we are talking about here. The liaison person is interested in linkages. He or she is concerned with creating relationships between the retarded citizen and the ecology. As we shall see in Chapter 8, the liaison role is perfectly complementary to the goals of systems-oriented psychological intervention. This role represents society's commitment to the idea that, historically, we have neglected the important construct of bad fit while concentrating too exclusively on bad people who come from bad environments (cf. Glidewell, 1972).

VALUES AND PUBLIC POLICY

The conclusion that science is not value free—indeed no understanding is value free—is one of the obvious and most important extensions of the transactional premise that the only reality we can ever have access to is that born of the involvement between a knower and that which is known. This point of view argues that we can have no objective understanding of anything because our understanding is always colored by our involvement with the phenomenon as we attempt to understand it. As we noted in previous chapters, our acts of observation always influence that which is observed.

Once having acknowledged that objective reality (or absolute truth) cannot be known in and of itself, independent of the knower, the scientist or observer must face squarely the issue of the value-laden aspects of science. There are several approaches one can take to the rational defense of the belief that science is not value-free. Each presentation of logical analysis will be different depending upon the choice of initial premises. As we noted in

Chapter 2, Capra begins with premises arising from the philosophy of science as considered within the context of modern subatomic physics.

> The crucial feature of quantum theory is that the observer is not only necessary to observe the properties of an atomic phenomenon, but is necessary even to bring about these properties. My conscious decision about how to observe, say an electron, will determine the electron's properties to some extent. If I ask it a particle question, it will give me a particle answer; if I ask it a wave question, it will give me a wave answer. The electron does not *have* objective properties independent of my mind. In atomic physics the sharp Cartesian division between mind and matter, between the observer and the observed, can no longer be maintained. We can never speak about nature without, at the same time, speaking about ourselves.
>
> In transcending the Cartesian division, modern physics has not only invalidated the classical ideal of an objective description of nature but has also challenged the myth of a value-free science. The patterns scientists observe in nature are intimately connected with the patterns of their minds; with their concepts, thoughts, and values. Thus the scientific results they obtain and the technological applications they investigate will be conditioned by their frame of mind. (1982, pp. 86–87)

Within community psychology, Paul Dokecki (1978, 1983) has written persuasively of the need to operate within a transactional perspective when conducting both science and practice; he cautions against the positivist view that science can be value-free. Dokecki does not substantiate his views through appeal to writings of the modern philosophical physicists. Rather, he acknowledges his debt (1983) to the theoretical and philosophical works of Perry London (1964), Gunnar Myrdal (1969), and Nicholas Hobbs (1975). Each of these social and psychological commentators has attempted to persuade that values must be articulated even when conducting enterprises such as science that, heretofore, have been thought to be bastions of the objective. For Dokecki, a recognition of the role of values in science leads quickly and inexorably to a consideration of public policy. If values are a part of scientific conduct and professional practice then public policy must be evaluated systematically and guided intentionally. With the French philosopher Paul Ricoeur (1978), he finds the most important value to be an insistence on protection of freedom — yours and mine. "*The supreme value is that I should be and that you should be.*" (Ricoeur, 1978, p. 180, italics added; Dokecki, 1983, p. 111) Dokecki and his colleagues (Hobbs et al., 1984) have derived a value analytic framework for public policy in psychology, for use particularly with issues related to communities and families. Intervention should be most basically concerned with enhancing development through community. The concept of community, as used here, reflects an investment in the ideas supporting the sense-of-community construct just presented. The aims of intervention should be to enhance community and human development.

The value analysis procedure outlined by Dokecki, Hobbs, and others call for policy makers to evaluate action in terms of a series of value elements. For example, the first value element for consideration asks if a given policy enhances community. Criteria within this framework include questions such as: Is it demeaning to any group? Does it bestow an unwarranted advantage? Is it divisive? Does it increase shared heritage, mutual aid, and community building?

This work presents a good example of how certain systemic notions can be extended in such a way that interesting, practical applications become possible across the broad array of interest areas within a subdiscipline, such as community psychology. In the past, there have been thinkers, good and bad, who intuited that values play a role in all human pursuits, even pursuits such as science, which seemed to be so objectively removed from the taint of human prejudices. A provocative knowledge base is beginning to become available and intuition and/or common sense no longer need to be relied on as heavily as before. Dokecki's work is reflective of an increasing number of theoreticians, scientists, and practitioners, who begin with systemic concepts and arrive at important conclusions.

5

FAMILIES: GOOD BEGINNINGS AND GOOD EXAMPLES

The power is only in the rules of the game.
— M. Selvini-Palazzoli

As the 1960s came to a close, Mara Selvini-Palazzoli, an Italian psychiatrist, found herself reviewing the cases of many anorexic children and their families, treated by her over the years. Her review was not favorable. After many hours of psychoanalytic treatment, the successes were few and the failures too frequent for professional and personal comfort. In response to a dismal situation, Selvini-Palazzoli organized a group of four psychiatrists into what became known as the Milan Associates: Luigi Boscolo, Gianfranco Cecchin, Giuliana Prata, and Selvini-Palazzoli herself. This group commandeered some of the ideas of Gregory Bateson (see Chapter 2), reworked them, developed an innovative model of practice consistent with the theory, began to change the lives of anorexic families in fewer than 15 sessions, and took the family therapy world by storm.

In the years since the Milan group's early work, their approach has been exported to other European countries and the Americas, where it has been further refined and tested. The most useful and intriguing examples of this approach to family therapy can be found in the original work of the Milan Associates and the writings and applied work of several psychotherapists associated with the New York-based Ackerman Institute at various times during the 1970s and 1980s: Lynn Hoffman, Brad Keeney, and Peggy Papp. For the most part, the Ackerman group owes an intellectual debt to Gregory Bateson as well as the Milan Associates; however, each takes a somewhat different approach to his or her systemic work, and each is worth considering in some detail.

Each of the approaches considered has weaknesses as well as strengths; thus, the reader is urged to consult all of the writers presented here. As a collection, the work is superb; broad understanding comes from approaching these particular writers as a group. A solid understanding of this important therepeutic approach must start with a consideration of its creation. Therefore, we begin by turning our attention toward Italy.

THE MILAN ASSOCIATES

In Selvini-Palazzoli's (1974) account of her review of the treatment of self starvation, she contrasted the intrapsychic approach with her newly developing model based on a view of the family as a system in which anorexia is an expression of the rules that govern the family's functioning. The Milan group began with a consideration of Selvini-Palazzoli's original work with anorexic families, then turned quickly to what they considered a more challenging system: the schizophrenic family. In 1978, this group of four psychoanalytically trained psychiatrists wrote *Paradox and Counterparadox: A New Model in the Therapy of the Family in Schizophrenic Transaction* (Selvini-Palazzoli, Cecchin, Prata, & Boscolo, 1978). Within five years, the book became a classic in the family therapy field and applications of the Milan approach could be found in all countries containing activity in applied psychology. The reason for such rapid interest and acceptance is simple but obvious: the Milan method worked. It constituted a fresh and fascinating approach to what had been a challenging and almost impossible task within the mental health fields: the effective treatment of schizophrenic families.

The label *systemic family therapy* originated with Selvini-Palazzoli and her colleagues. The central hypothesis for their work has been that "the family is a self-regulating system which controls itself according to rules formed over a period of time through a process of trial and error" (Selvini-Palazzoli et al., 1978, p. 3). As the family group transacts across time, the members communicate verbally and nonverbally, constantly creating feedback loops— patterns, if you will. Schizophrenic behavior in one member of the family constitutes a pattern that emerges from the family communication loops. It is not the identified patient who is schizophrenic. It just looks that way. It is the family, the system, that more appropriately can be thought of as schizophrenic. These families are held together by communication patterns that represent the rules that control the system. The set of rules that govern the family in schizophrenic transaction is complex and hidden from the conscious awareness of family members. The Milan group has identified a general set of rules within which most schizophrenic families operate, each in its own unique way.

These scientist-practitioners agree with Bowen (1960) that an identified schizophrenic person is the product of at least three generations. Behavioral rigidity has become apparent by the second generation and family members are quite fearful of rejection. Thus, the bid for *confirmation* is an intense one, which has little chance of fulfillment because giving approval is a sign of weakness in this system. From the point of view of a family member,

> if someone does something well, it is clear that he only does so in order to receive praise or approval. In such a case, the rendering of approval or praise would mean giving in to his expectations, putting oneself "down," and sustaining a loss of prestige and authority. To maintain this position of prestige and authority, it is necessary to withhold approval, to find something to criticize or make fun of: "Yes, but you could have done better'; 'Fine, but the next time . . .'." (Selvini-Palazzoli et al., 1978, p. 23)

Another rule involves the need to increase the amount of the punished or uncomfortable behavior as a means of *verifying the existence of the rule*. The Milan group thinks of this as a "consequence of a person's finding himself 'down' when he has tried to be 'up' in the effort to define the relationship. Let it be clear that we are not talking about the effort to control other persons, but rather about the effort to control the *relationship*" (p. 24, italics added).

Disqualifying one's own definition of the relationship before risking disqualification of it by the other is another important rule that governs the system. Such a maneuver might involve statements such as, "I don't really need it from you. I just felt like saying that." Or, "I've never thought of you as my sister anyway." Other communicational rules involve "*partial or total disqualification of the message, sidestepping of the main issue, change of subject, non sequitur, amnesia*, and finally the supreme maneuver of *disconfirmation*. . . . " (p. 25, italics added).

Disconfirmation can be manifested in one of two ways. In the first, a family member indicates that the other does not really exist for him or her. In an even more powerful dynamic, the person communicates that, "I am not really here. You have no one to relate to. I don't exist for you." No matter which communication pattern is controlling system functioning at a given time, a fundamental proscription against leaving the field is always present. With logic that is quite reminiscent of the Bateson work discussed earlier, the Milan group believes the cardinal rule to be that each person is free to threaten to leave the relationship, the family, the city, even life itself—but no one may actually break off from the system. Even marriage of a child may not result in leaving; often the couple moves into the parental home, the apartment overhead, into grandmother's house, and so forth.

Much of the 1978 work written by Selvini-Palazzoli and her colleagues contains detailed descriptions of the ways in which families in schizophrenic transaction interpret these rules in creative and unique ways. As the group notes, "The repertoire of moves is infinite and one rule of the game is: Anything goes. Eroticism, incest, infidelity, hostility, affectionate indulgence, dependence, independence, boredom (with the game), interest (elsewhere), etc., etc." (p. 29). This material is scattered throughout the Milan group's book and is worth reading simply for the vivid picture it presents of life within the schizophrenic system. Despite the potency of these descriptions, the most enduring merit of the work and the freshest part of the approach lies not in its presentation of the rules that govern the family caught in schizophrenic transaction, but the rules that govern the operation of the therapists committed to systemic therapy.

The Theory and the Method

In order for the therapy to be effective, the Milan group cautions that you must become aware that when beginning with a schizophrenic family, you are entering a game. All power is located solely in the rules of the game and it is the communication patterns that are, themselves, the rules. The only major goal of systemic therapy is to change the rules of the game. Locating and changing one fundamental rule can change the family; the schizophrenic transactions can be dramatically altered. The theoretical argument supporting belief in this postulate can be found in the thinking of most of the writers we have considered in previous chapters. The argument is based on the belief that changing a fundamental part changes the whole: *if you change one important rule, you change the entire game.* By way of analogy, consider the effect on the game of football if the rule concerning the playing field were changed, say, to indicate that it be played in a 100-yard-long swimming pool. Or, what happens if the political game called *presidential election* undergoes one major rule change that calls for the election to occur every 25 years rather than every 4 years. In both cases, we end up playing a very different game. And, so it is with the schizophrenic family who cannot sustain an attack on a fundamental family communication rule.

The systemic therapists plot their strategies as if they were playing the most elegant game of chess with the region's most skillful player. As one reads their work, it is easy to develop a picture of a team of good-natured therapists aiming at the family's jugular vein (as it were). The jugular vein in this case is referred to as the *nodal point.* In general systems theory, Ps, the nodal point, is thought of as the point at which an optimal number of functions within a system converge. Alteration of a nodal point results in alteration of the system. Using our football and presidential election examples, it becomes easy enough to see that the change in one fundamental rule brings with it an inevitable change in all the rest. Picture for a moment the game of football played in water. Imagine the alterations, additions, subtractions and so forth that would be required of *all* other rules. Consideration of the changes surrounding the necessary change in appropriate wearing apparel is, by itself, enough to boggle the mind.

When listening to members of the Milan group and when reading their work, it becomes quickly apparent that they have a very substantial amount of respect for schizophrenic family members and for the rules of the schizophrenic game. These therapists are professionals and like any good athletic professional they appreciate a good opponent. They talk of laughing when they are outwitted and of reacting with awe at the incredible creativity of some of the moves.

Rather than blaming a family member who seems to have hamstrung the forward momentum of the therapeutic process, the team seems to develop an almost jovial appreciation of the prowess of that particular player. It is possible for Selvini-Palazzoli and her associates to develop this stance toward their clients because they are committed theoretically to a systemic understanding of the family in schizophrenic transaction. Within this model, causal attributions are disregarded. Newtonian reliance on the explanatory utility of causality is quite noticeably absent. The Milan group believes that

> we must abandon the causal-mechanistic view of phenomena, which has dominated the sciences until recent times, and adopt a systemic orientation. With this new orientation, the therapist should be able to see the members of the family as elements in a circuit of interaction. None of the members of the circuit have undirectional power over the whole, although the behavior of any one of the members inevitably influences the behavior of the others. At the same time, it is epistemologically incorrect to consider the behavior of one individual the *cause* of the behavior of the others. This is because every member influences the others, but is in turn influenced by them. The individual acts upon the system, but is at the same time influenced by the communications he receives from it. (Selvini-Palazzoli et al., 1978, p. 5)

Adoption of this premise means that systemic therapists do not interpret things in terms such as "His passivity causes her to act out"; "The girl's rejection of affection causes the mother to blame and hate herself"; "When he comes after her, she is forced to fight back." *Within this model, there is no search for causes. There is only a search for the rules that govern the action.*

Reliance on causal interpretation of life experiences is deeply ingrained in Western culture. The typical Western person is quite sure that causality really exists in the world and that successful living can only happen when causal sequences can be predicted and then controlled. If I can figure out that you will be forced to fire me if I exhibit a certain behavior, I am in a position to prevent the firing. If I can further discover what behaviors will cause you to promote me and give me a pay raise, so much the better. The smart person in Western society is the one who can figure out what will cause what to happen — and what can prevent it. Those who control the causes are those who control the world. Because this belief is woven so tightly throughout the patterns of our thought, it is difficult to develop an acausal way of viewing things. It is particularly difficult when one has entered the web of schizophrenic communication patterns within a family.

Surely this is one of the most difficult arenas in which to practice changing the cultural legacy of a couple of thousand years. Yet, the Milan group gave it a try—and pulled it off. To a great extent, their success at altering their causal modes of thinking is due to the ingenious therapy methods that developed as extensions of the theory. For example, the decision to use a team of four therapists with each family provided the opportunity for the breakdown of traditional reliance on causal interpretation.

In the Milan method, two therapists are present in the room with the family and two therapists are located behind a one-way mirror. The family is aware of therapeutic observers and is told that these therapists will participate from time to time by calling one therapist (or both) from the room in order to make suggestions or to correct any mistakes the therapists might be making. The therapy session is preceded by a session in which strategies are planned and it is followed by another session in which the family also is not present. Subsequent to this third component, the therapists return to the room and offer comments and prescriptions to the family. Much of the focus of the intrateam discussion is on the need to avoid assigning blame. There are continual reminders to abandon the automatic tendency to search for causes. Success occurs as the team ferrets out a fundamental rule of communication, not a specific cause for a specific behavior (or host of behaviors, for that matter).

Language is, of course, one of the biggest problems. Selvini-Palazzoli and her colleagues write that

> Since language is descriptive and linear, we are forced, in order to describe a transaction, to use a dichotomization or to introduce a series of dichotomizations. The dichotomization which we are forced to use by the very nature of language, requiring a "before" and "after," a subject and object (in the sense of he who *performs* the action and he who *receives* the action), implies a postulate of cause and effect, and, in consequence, a moralistic definition. (Selvini-Palazzoli, 1978, pp. 52-53)

Systemic therapists are armed with an emerging set of fresh perspectives on the nature of reality and the functioning of human groups. They are also armed with old languages; and these languages are heavily dependent on conceptions of causality, linearity, deduction, objects, and so forth. The Western languages are not able to capture adequately the true potential of ideas that concern unity, pattern, function, circularity and relationship. It is here, too, that the uniqueness of systemic strategies pays off; the methods help to circumvent the deficiencies of language.

Initial strategies are geared toward identification of a communication pattern, a rule, which can serve as an appropriate target of intervention. Almost immediately, further strategies are designed to have an impact upon that pattern. While a variety of novel strategies has been identified and reported by the Milan Associates, the most famous—and probably most used — is the maneuver of introducing a counterparadox into a paradoxical situation. The strategy has been so influential that the concept of paradox in relation to counterparadox is captured in the title of the Milan group's 1978 book. When describing the general paradoxical situation binding the family in schizophrenic transaction, these theoreticians give us a compelling introduction to the thought processes themselves. They share with us the family member's reasoning that

> Only if you were not what you are can I be what I am not but what I should have been. To help me you don't have to do anything, it wouldn't help anyway. In order to really help me, you should really *be* what you should have been. . . ." Thus we can formulate the schizophrenic message: "It's not that you should *do* something different; you should *be* different. Only in this way can you help me to be what I'm not, but what I could be if you were not what you are. (Selvini-Palazzoli, 1978, p. 36)

The variations on this theme are probably limitless. Each interpretation of it, however, functionally provides the same consequences for family dynamics: it prevents change. Family therapists speak of this as a homeostatic condition. The family players are stuck, and thus obliged to endlessly repeat well-worn communication patterns. In order to interrupt this cycle, systemic therapists identify a crucial family communication rule, inevitably finding that it represents a paradoxical set of instructions. Recall the Bateson examples (Chapter 2) of children from schizophrenic families, who quickly learn that they are damned if they do and equally damned if they do not.

After deciding on an appropriate target rule, the Selvini group attempts to "jam the system"; that is, they deliberately make it impossible for the rule to continue to function in critical therapeutic moments. Often, this is best accomplished by introducing a counterparadox. For example, in a situation where a child expects emotional punishment for loving a parent and equally severe emotional punishment for failing to do so, a typical systemic strategy might be to *positively connote* the child's bizarre dinner time behavior by telling the family something to the effect of: "Johnny senses his mother's pain from the cruel treatment she has received at the hands of her own parents and her husband's parents and he knows she is confused as to how she wishes him to respond to her. Since she was never treated fairly she does not know how to expect a child of her own—who is treated well—to behave. Knowing this, and caring for his mother, Johnny acts up every night at dinner so that his mother can blame him and not herself. Johnny serves the family well by these outbursts. He makes it possible for his mother not to hate herself. Therefore, Johnny—who is doing the right thing—should continue these outbursts for at least 15 minutes during every mealtime for the next 30 days. He may take a break on Sunday evenings if he chooses. If he and his mother see no need for an outburst on Sunday night then he is permitted to decide against having one. It is entirely up to him. We can only be impressed at the level of commitment Johnny has to the family and we feel sure that his judgment can be trusted in this matter."

The Milan Associates do not predict the specific results of an intervention such as this. Rather, they predict that the family will need to move to a new level of communication in order to deal with the counterparadox with which they have been presented. In the most positive of circumstances, they will move to the level of metacommunication; that is, they will talk about the *process* of communication in the family — an almost nonexistent occurrence in schizophrenic families. No matter what happens, the important thing is that something different happens. A family communication rule gets changed. And that is the beginning of system reorganization. It is possible that major change could occur within the therapeutic hour or within just a few sessions of practicing the "prescription." In fact, the Milan Associates have most often contracted for only 10 sessions with a family, usually a month apart. Not only have they reported remarkable change, they have reported quick change.

While the Milan group has described sudden changes, they have not offered any detailed or robust theory to account for them. In addition to an absence of conventional outcome research, this lack of explanatory theory supporting the reported rapid changes associated with the Milan approach constitutes one of its biggest weaknesses. Fortunately, others have spent time with this phenomenon and have valuable insights to offer. Lynn Hoffman has been one of those who has seriously addressed this issue.

THE HOFFMAN APPROACH

In the early 1980s several major interpretations of the Milan work became available in this country. The most important were authored by psychotherapists associated at one time or another with the Ackerman Institute in New York. Lynn Hoffman (1981) produced the first of these, only three years after the publication of the Selvini-Palazzoli et al. work. Among the products coming out of Ackerman, Hoffman's has been considered by many to be the best. Indeed, it was somewhat common in the early 1980s to hear her book referred to as "Lynn Hoffman's beautiful book." If Hoffman's work is superior, it is most probably because it is so readable. Systemic family therapists have been particularly aware of the difficulties created when using conventional Western language in the attempt to illustrate systemic thought. As a result of the desire to communicate in a precise fashion, a language has grown up with the movement that is sometimes difficult for the lay person to comprehend. Hoffman has been able to capture and present systemic language and at the same time to communicate clearly to the uninitiated reader.

As I have commented elsewhere (Plas, 1985), *Foundations of Family Ther-*

apy is a misleading title for the Hoffman book. Her work does not constitute a detailed presentation of the variety of approaches to family therapy in use today. Rather, it tilts decidedly in the direction of the systemic approach. Nonetheless, the reader who is unfamiliar with the full range of theory and practice in family therapy is urged to consult the Hoffman book. Her descriptions of the leading therapies and therapists is comprehensive and fair; the reader who is particularly interested in the systemic points of view will find the presentation particularly helpful, since she attempts to relate these to the full range of practice available for those interested in working with families.

Hoffman is pretty thoroughly Batesonian, although the influence of Maturana has reached her through her attention to the systemic writings of Paul Dell (1981; 1982), an interpreter of the Maturana thinking in this country. The philosophical concept of epistemology (see Chapter 2) is an important one for Hoffman. While the Milan group has used the construct, they have used it sparingly; Hoffman moves it to a position of centrality.

Epistemology—the study of how knowledge occurs, how we come to know anything—is of premier importance. The strength of her allegiance to this notion is great.

> What I believe we are witnessing is the emergence of a second generation of family therapists clearly distinguishable from the first. This second generation is not content with just a change in etiology. To say that "The family, not the individual, is the 'cause' of the problem" is not a real change for them. They are grasping the real meaning of Bateson's thought, and they are understanding what the strategic theorists in Palo Alto, the systemic practitioners in Milan, and other voices in the United States and Europe have been trying to convey: the need for a new epistemology. This new epistemology would influence profoundly not only the way one thought about therapy but also how one practiced it. (Hoffman, 1981, p. 345)

Discontinuous Change

Hoffman turns to physicists Prigogine (1980) and Platt (1970) as well as Bateson and Maturana, as she attempts to develop a practical theoretical explanation of the experience of sudden change within families involved in systemic treatment. These scientists have been associated with interesting and innovative research in other fields, designed in large part as a test of the hypotheses that discontinuous change is to be expected within living systems under certain sets of circumstances. Leaps to a new level of organization occur as fluctuations in previously stable patterns become amplified. These changes appear to be system-generated and irreversible; they are often dramatic.

As Hoffman develops this theme for the field of family therapy, she importantly reminds us that living systems are predisposed toward change. A healthy living system strains toward the next evolutionary stage. Evolving, vital family systems create changing patterns of communication rather automatically. While such changes are by no means pain-free in the typical growing family, they are nonetheless healthy and inevitable. A family in schizophrenic transaction is caught in a static condition where the rules governing the system are locked into seemingly hopeless redundancies. Hoffman helps us to see the energy that is part of the schizophrenic system. She suggests that the static communication patterns in these families seem to have blinded us to the potentialities for change. She points out that the energy that holds the redundancies in place is available for system transformation. A sense of hope rather than hopelessness is conveyed in Hoffman's writing. The family in schizophrenic transaction almost seems to be a more accommodating intervention target than the typical healthy family already engaged in evolutionary change. The energy is bound up within the schizophrenic system. If the energy can be released, it can rather quickly create a leap to a new level of organization, a new level of family communication. Another term for this phenomenon, *hierarchical growth*, helps to capture the evolutionary essence of the concept. Hoffman describes the stages of the process.

> The natural history of a leap or transformation is usually this: First, the patterns that have kept the system in a steady state relative to its environment begin to work badly. New conditions arise for which these patterns were not designed. Ad hoc solutions are tried and sometimes work, but usually have to be abandoned. Irritation grows over small but persisting difficulties. The accumulation of dissonance eventually forces the entire system over an edge, into a state of crisis, as the stabilizing tendency brings on ever-intensifying corrective sweeps that get out of control. The end point of what cybernetic engineers call a runaway is that the system breaks down, or creates a new way to monitor the same homeostasis, or spontaneously leaps to an integration that will deal better with the changed field. (Hoffman, 1981, pp. 159–160)

Since a transformative leap to a better level of functioning is by no means assured, systemic strategies must be geared toward identification of a point of impact, a nodal point, that will maximize probabilities of success. The introduction of systemic therapy creates new possibilities, for it adds something to the system. This approach introduces strategies geared toward helping a targeted communication rule to begin fluctuating such that conditions are put in place for the possibility of the sudden leap.

In her efforts to evoke positive change, Hoffman has had greatest success with the strategy of introducing what she calls a "simple bind." Essentially, she is talking about the Milan group's counterparadoxical move. The reader with an interest in the specifics of systemic therapy is urged to consult Hoffman's writings on the topic of the simple bind. Not only does she sensitively portray the plight of a "stuck" family, she addresses in a practical fashion the plight of the systemic therapist who does not wish to harm a family with a maladaptive prescription. Hoffman walks the therapist through a series of danger signals to be on the lookout for as the process of therapy proceeds.

When reading Hoffman one begins to get a sense for what this somewhat elusive new way of thinking is all about. Truly, she believes that she is reporting on an epistemological revolution that finds old notions of linear causality to be misleading at best. Like the Selvini group, Hoffman seems genuinely to like her clients. Obviously, the elimination of the need to blame the one or the many gives us a new ability as people and as therapists to take a fresher look at what is before us. When we do not blame, it is easier to appreciate and to love.

KEENEY AND CYBERNETICS

Another Ackerman Institute therapist, Brad Keeney, interprets systemic family therapy from the point of view of cybernetics. For Keeney (1983), this term describes a way of viewing things that is part of a general science concerned with patterns and ordering. He is chiefly interested in helping us change our methods of observation so as to look at patterns rather than the material, to look at process and ordering rather than objects. A purist emphasis on this point results in a push to have us ignore the whole as well as the parts, to see nothing but that which is referred to with terms such as *pattern, organization, order, redundancy,* and so forth.

Keeney's intellectual indebtedness is principally to Gregory Bateson, Maturana and Varella, and cyberneticist Heinz von Foerster (1973; 1976). Keeney's love affair with the concept of epistemology is even more obvious than Hoffman's; perhaps as a result, his explanations of the meaning and uses of the construct are even more comprehensive and compelling than hers.

Within the field of philosophy, a person's epistemological stance reflects his or her assumptions concerning how knowing occurs, the rules governing it, and its limits. Keeney writes that, "In the sociocultural domain, epistemology becomes a study of how people or systems of people know things and how they think they know things" (1983, p. 13). No matter what the philosophical persuasion, most philosophers would agree that everyone has an epistemology. Each of us has a set of assumptions about how we and others are able to know anything at all and each of us has a set of beliefs about what is impossible for us to ever know given the rules as we understand them. Of course, we need not be consciously aware that we have an epistemology in order for it to work for us.

The existence of functioning epistemological beliefs is of crucial importance in any consideration of reality. Some would say that the very reality we see is created through, or influenced by, or dependent upon, our beliefs concerning what it is possible to see. This fundamental point is one that is appreciated by the Milan group, Hoffman, and Keeney, as well as Bateson, Capra, Maturana, and the others whose thinking is relied on by the systemic psychologists. A problematic issue relative to this whole thing, however, is that while the concept is vital, it is a sticky one to grasp and present in a clear and meaningful fashion. Keeney does a nice job of attacking the issue head on; although, probably, for many readers he does not quite get the job done. If one has a grasp of cybernetic thought and is quite conversant with the work of Bateson and one or two of the others mentioned here, Keeney reads elegantly on this point. He sheds light on some of the more murky issues and pushes off in provocative new directions. However, for those who are new to this method of thinking, his writing can be problematic. An abstract of his thought concerning the fundamental importance of epistemology will follow. The reader who is newly involved with this material is encouraged to consider the issue again when it is introduced in detail in Chapter 6.

Keeney finds himself, like all systemic writers, somewhat perplexed by the limitations of language and his allegiance to the epistemological belief that what we are able to know depends on the world view we are using as we attempt to know it. It seems a bit like one of Bateson's double binds, doesn't it? It is at least reminiscent of a classic paradox. Keeney asserts that

> Epistemology is more fundamental than the action and ideas most clinicians describe. One simply cannot clearly describe an alternative epistemology in conventional terms any more than a sorcerer can describe an alternative world of experience to an uninitiated outsider.
>
> The roadblock for the reader is that no school of therapy, sequence of action, or collection of metaphors can be provided to concretely illustrate an alternative epistemology. What one sees will always be shaped by the world in which one is presently operating. To view an alternative world requires being in that world. Thus, the most this text can do is prescribe various paths for encountering an alternative epistemology and then warn of the possibility that each of these paths may be twisted and distorted by the world view of which one is already part. . . . the "world of transition" is a fuzzy one. Being in transition from one epistemology to another means moving toward seeing a world that, by definition, is impossible to grasp in the world to which one is traditionally accustomed. (Keeney, 1983, p. 15)

Systemic epistemology holds that *what* we know is necessarily dependent upon *how* we know. One of the methods Keeney uses to illustrate the reality of this assumption as he understands it is through discussion of the concept of "distinction." Following a line of thinking proposed by others (cf. Spencer-Brown, 1973), he finds it making sense that the first thing we do as knowers is to draw distinctions between things, or processes, or whatever. As I glance up from my writing at the moment, I distinguish Ruby, my secretary, from the file cabinet, from the piece of paper in her hand, and so on. I could, if I had reason to do so, distinguish her from other women I have known, other secretaries, taller people, or those with less of a sense of humor. Distinctions, you see, are made across time as well as space.

Because Ruby has conveniently remained within my field of vision, I can use the moment to illustrate further Keeney's point concerning distinctions. I note that I can distinguish rapid arm movements from slower ones; a smile from a neutral expression; redness as opposed to whiteness or greenness; sound from silence. I have taken two quite different views of the same occurrence. A visitor from Western Samoa would undoubtedly distinguish very different things; other phenomena would be separated, pulled apart for inspection and knowing. An organism from another galaxy might not distinguish my dear Ruby at all. We distinguish based on the equipment we possess as human beings and on the basis of our world view. Thus, the very reality we describe is inseparable from the way we approach the description. Keeney points out that: "The observer first distinguishes and then describes. A question, by proposing a distinction, constructs its answer" (p. 20). Language participates in the creation of the reality it attempts to describe. Keeney has referred to language as an "epistemological knife" (p. 110).

The epistemology which Keeney's own world view relies on is a cybernetic, or systemic one, which considers the knower to be heavily represented in that which becomes known. Therefore, a systemic therapist attempts to view the therapeutic event in terms of patterns and patterns which connect (cf. Bateson, 1979, for a full consideration of the pattern which connects). A view of separation between therapist and client or family member and family member ought to be avoided. Keeney tells us that "the map is always in the territory, the observer in the observed, the therapist in the system being treated" (p. 130). Elsewhere he states that

> The way in which a therapist is part of feedback will lead to particular ways in which family members organize their behavior around him. Their reactions, however, lead the therapist to organizing his behavior around them, and so on, round and round.
> From the perspective of cybernetics, the most a therapist can do is vary his behavior, recognize the subsequent behavior of those in the surrounding social field, and modify his reactions to their reactions. If the effects of his behavior on others are used, in turn, to change his behavior, feedback is established. The therapist is not controlling their behavior, but is recognizing the response of their behavior to his and the response of his behavior to theirs. (Keeney, 1983, pp. 132-133)

This way of thinking and set of conclusions is problematic for some and ridiculous to others; a third group, the systemic therapists, find it useful. The position described suggests to those who begin with assumptions different from Keeney that he has abdicated his responsibility as a therapist; or, even worse, he doesn't understand that his behavior *does* cause his clients to respond, that he indeed *can* control behavior under certain circumstances.

Keeney's systems-oriented views find him believing that a therapist — a bad or a good one — cannot control behavior or elicit responses. Rather, a good therapist knows how to vary his or her own behavior, is adept at seeing a variety of patterns of action, can recognize redundancies, and at all times recognizes that the system being observed includes the therapist's self as well as other selves. Further, the good therapist "knows" that his or her descriptions are colored by the cultural and personal background of the therapist, his or her language and world view.

Keeney's chapters are comprehensive and stimulating. In most cases, he carries a point to its logical extreme no matter what sacred cows get in the way. This is a much-needed explanatory strategy in this field. Readability is crucial but so is the effort to push a point beyond the average reader's ability to remain interested in the topic. This is new ground and does not get broken without sweat and aggravation; both Hoffman and Keeney have realized this.

THE PAPP INTERPRETATION

Peggy Papp visited the Milan program in 1974, before publication of the group's seminal volume. She returned to the Ackerman Institute to direct, with Olga Silverstein, what became known as the Brief Therapy Project. Among those discussed here, Papp's writings tend to be the most eclectic. In her 1983 book, *The Process of Change*, she evidences allegience to therapeutic approaches other than the systemic, notably that of Jay Haley (1963; 1973). However, the Milan influence on her work has been direct and pervasive.

Papp is a pragmatist. She admits that if it works, she uses it; and, the basics of the Milan approach work for her. Her writing is as straightforward as her intentions. Like other systems-oriented writers, she struggles with the complexities involved in trying to grasp and clearly present ideas that do not lend themselves to conventional Western language. To a great extent she succeeds. However, her book is not heavily devoted to lengthy explications of theory. She concentrates on method and carefully explains why she, as therapist, does what she does.

Papp begins with an explanation of the basic concept of system by offering the following observation:

> Most trainees respond to an academic explanation of a family system with a dazed look, as though to say: "So what does one do with a self-corrective, homeostatic system which is error activated and regulates itself through negative and positive feedback loops in order to maintain its equilibrium?" (a cybernetic definition of a system). Or: "How does one deal with a unit with an internal design which evolves to new and unpredictable levels of organization through the process of discontinuous change and unpredictable leaps?" (an evolutionary definition of a system). (Papp, 1983, p. 6)

In the first of these definitions, she gives a Keeney-like view of system while the second is more complementary with Hoffman's approach. The entire passage reflects Papp's sensitivity to the need for clear and quick communication. Hers is basically a book on method. The theory is there but it occasionally needs to be teased from fascinating case examples, which find the reader smiling appreciatively at her clinical artistry.

A good example of Papp's ability to synthesize and communicate can be found in her description of the theoretical elements that deserve attention:

> The key concepts of systems thinking have to do with wholeness, organization, and patterning. Events are studied within the context in which they are occurring, and attention is focused on connections and relationships rather than on individual characteristics. The central ideas of this theory are that the whole is considered to be greater than the sum of its parts; each part can only be understood in the context of the whole; a change in any one part will affect every other part; and the whole regulates itself through a series of feedback loops that are referred to as cybernetic circuits. Information loops travel back and forth within these feedback loops in order to provide stability or homeostasis for the system. The parts are constantly changing in order to keep the system balanced (as a tightrope walker constantly shifts his/her weight to preserve equilibrium). The overall system maintains its shape as the pattern of linkage between the parts changes. This concept of patterning and circular organization, as opposed to individual description and linear explanation, has become the foundation upon which family therapy rests. (Papp, 1983, p. 7)

This passage provides a sense of her roots outside of systemic thought as well as a glimpse into her communication style. For example, some of the systems-oriented thinkers Papp finds useful prefer to think of all systems as in a state of balance rather than in a state of flux and change. That view clearly comes through in the interpretation of key concepts noted earlier. Pragmatically, Papp comments later that the issue of homeostatic vs. dynamic models is not an important one for her. What is important is that systems and symptoms serve one another. In a fascinating and useful section describing the functioning of family symptoms and the covariates of symptom elimination, Papp cogently comments that

> The central therapeutic issue is not how to eliminate the symptom but what will happen if it is eliminated; the therapeutic argument is shifted from the problem, who has it, what caused it, and how to get rid of it, to how the family will function without it, what price will have to be paid for its removal, who will pay it, and whether it is worth it. (Papp, 1983, p. 13)

This kind of theoretical understanding is potent; it is usually the result of years of experience. Since Papp has been practicing for 20-odd years, experience is one of the main ingredients her interpretation has to offer.

There are excellent discussions here on clinical hypothesis formation, setting the terms for therapy, and negotiating change. Many case presentations are available, as is a good chapter on failures and pitfalls. Of greatest importance for our discussion, however, is the adaptation of the Milan strategy for which Papp has perhaps become best known: the Greek Chorus.

The Greek Chorus

Like the Milan Associates, the Brief Therapy Project uses a consultation group behind the one-way mirror. If family members wish to meet the members of the group, that is arranged. However, no direct negotiation with these therapists is possible for the family. As Papp puts it, they remain "a prophetic voice: unapproachable, unimpeachable, and unnegotiable" (p. 46). Often, a therapeutic triangle is formed, with the group behind the mirror functioning as the villains who offer all manner of reasons why particular family symptoms ought not to be changed. Creating a division between the therapists in the room and those out of the room constitutes an important divergence from the method of operation in Milan. Despite this difference, the reader most often sees similarities since Papp, like Selvini-Palazzoli and her colleagues, sets for her teams the major task of discovering the rules of the game. Donald Bloch (in Papp, 1983) has noted that the Greek Chorus forms one of the methods used by Papp to create "a structure in the therapeutic team that is isomorphic to the nodal, symptom-related pattern in the family" (p. xi).

IN RETROSPECT

Bloch, director of the Ackerman Institute, has been in a unique position to observe the various transformations of the original Milan approach that have emanated from the Ackerman clinical setting. He has commented that

> The interesting difference from the Milan practice lies in the Italian adherence to a highly formal and invariant presentation of the group (at least in their earlier work), along with a personal style that minimizes involvement and affective expression. The Americans, by contrast, are not above hyperbole and dramatic gesture in the interest of eliciting an enactment. (Papp, 1983. p. xi)

Until additional research is forthcoming, we are presumably free to choose either of these interpretations: the Italian version or the more Americanized approach. The Milan strategies have never relied on the idea of the charismatic therapist. In fact, a goal has been to structure the method so that it can operate effectively through any trained therapist. Emotion coming from the therapist is rarely needed nor risked. Some of the American versions do use the emotional energy of the therapist. At this point, it is, perhaps, a matter of taste.

It is important to note here that for each of the writers presented, the main focus is on the rules of system, not on causality or blame. In addition, theory is critical, respected, and used. The combination of these two points allows systemic therapists to treat their client families with respect — to even enjoy them. Technique without theory, and attention to causes rather than rules, would find systemic therapists acting as simple manipulators rather than helping professionals who possess the capacity to care.

6

SYSTEMIC FUNDAMENTALS: A LIST

Fundamental progress has to do with the reinterpretation of basic ideas.
— A. N. Whitehead

Before considering systemic approaches designed for classrooms and schools, we need to list the fundamentals of a systemic approach. Unfortunately, such lists have been hard to find. As noted earlier, systems-oriented thinking is relatively new to the fields of psychology and education, the process of systemic thinking is not a particularly easy one for the conventional Western mind, and those who offer systemic thought to the social sciences have, for the most part, caught hold of these newer ideas by way of the physical sciences, each of which takes a slightly different approach to the issues and empirical work. For these and other reasons, a list of the components of a systemic perspective cannot be found in most of the current major texts on this topic. Fundamental principles can be teased from the presentations but that process can become lamentably tedious at times. Understandably, it was not possible to articulate concisely a list of major points during the systemic movement's infancy. Participation in constructing a new world view has historically required dialogue, incubation, and time.

Largely, one will find a similar group of fundamentals referred to by each systemic writer. However, given the variety of routes taken to arrive at an appreciation of the possibilities inherent in systems psychology, it is not surprising that each writer tends to emphasize a select group of points, sometimes at the expense of others. The following list of fundamentals is probably no exception. Time may reveal it to be less comprehensive than desirable; however, it should prove currently useful — perhaps simply because it *is* a list, a gathering of those points that seem to deserve at least tentative status as postulates. Thus, the list represents one systemic thinker's understanding of those perspectives necessary to a description of a systemic approach. Each of these perspectives has been referenced several times in previous chapters; each has been considered crucial by the majority of writers considered here. Thus, the reader will find the ideas familiar at this point.

While each idea is reviewed rather than introduced in this chapter, in most instances, additional ways of thinking about a given issue are included. In each case, suggestions for developing a systemic way of thinking follow presentation of the basic idea.

This set of points has been culled from the work of early transactional and Gestalt psychologists as well as contemporary family therapists. Major indebtedness, then, is to Gregory Bateson, John Dewey and Arthur Bentley, and interpreters of the Milan approach to family therapy. A definition of systemic psychology follows consideration of each of the fundamental postulates. These basic perspectives derive from consideration of the crucial issues of language, epistemology, linearity, causality, forms of reasoning, wholes, patterns and rules, dynamic models, discontinuous change, and stories. All of these issues are interconnected. At times, it gets a bit tricky to talk about one of them in isolation from the rest. In almost all cases, it is necessary to try to do so, however. The ideas are somewhat foreign to our traditional Western minds and it is profitable to focus exclusively on a new notion as we begin to learn to use it. Some of the labels contained in the list have a systemic flavor (e.g., patterns and rules), while others are couched in more conventional Western terms (e.g., causality), and still others are more epistemologically neutral in form (e.g., forms of reasoning). The reason for this variety, of course, is that the English language is not prepared to support some of the ideas with which we are concerned here. Therefore, it will be wise to begin with a discussion of the role of language.

LANGUAGE

Linguist Benjamin Whorf (1941) declared that the very realities of persons cannot be the same unless their languages are the same or can be calibrated in some way. In an important sense, reality is a language-made affair. This is a bold declaration. In various forms, it has been supported by many reputable thinkers (cf. Berger & Luckmann, 1967; Langer, 1942; 1962). However, it has been ignored or ridiculed elsewhere, notably by the typical person in the street. The idea that language creates reality in some sense, rather than simply reflecting it, is utter nonsense on first apprehension. A tree exists whether I call it a "tree" or whether I call it an "eert." Whorf's notion must be wrong, then, for the very realities of people must always be identical no matter what names their particular language gives to things. Common sense has difficulty with the idea that language participates in reality-making, and common sense is the sharpest mental tool available to the most demanding intellectual critic in Western history: the information flooded average contemporary person.

Yet, it is precisely these people—you and I, for example—who lament the distortion of language within contemporary political and marketing practices. The perversion of the language wreaks havoc on our understandings of reality. We seem to sense this fact, sometimes hopelessly and sometimes with a bit of anger. In a world that finds the large size, the economy size, and the king size all being the *same* size (usually a pretty small size), it is time, from a purely practical standpoint, to take a look at the contributions of language to reality. Those who have been pursuing a systems perspective have been engaged in this language business for some 30 to 40 years now, building on the history of Western philosophy as well as developments in contemporary physical science and an appreciation of Eastern ways of thinking about the world. Their conclusions are very interesting, indeed.

During the first half of this century, John Dewey and Arthur Bentley shared with others the common assumption that the goal of scientific inquiry is the understanding or "knowing" of target realities. Thus, the goal of science is to understand the tree, the stars, electricity, genetic structure, the contribution of vitamins to the developing human and, perhaps, even the function (if not the nature) of love and hate in the world. Unlike most of their contemporaries, however, Dewey and Bentley believed that to name is to know. They felt that naming and knowing—language and understanding, if you will—were twin aspects of the same phenomenon. Having read the early work in quantum mechanics, they drew the conclusion that observer and observed were inseparable, with language representing the transaction between the two.

If you, two friends, an interplanetary visitor, a Sioux Indian grandmother, a Swiss goatherd, and a Brazilian coffee grinder were each to be placed in a room empty of everything except a chair and a table supporting an object quite foreign to all of you, each of you would describe the object in a different way. If you were permitted no access to human conversation and were required for six months to study the object in any way you chose, with whatever sophisticated equipment you might commandeer or dream up, imagine the extent of the difference between your verbal description and that of the Sioux grandmother or Swiss goatherd. Let us presume even further that the interplanetary visitor might produce the most unrecognizable reality of all. What should we make of these discrepancies? Those who emphasize the role of language would have us understand that the languages we come equipped with reflect the most basic difference. They hold that our language mirrors our very understanding of reality. The word *atom*, for example, reflects a construct. Each of us who has the word *atom* in our vocabulary has hold of that construct to some extent. Because of that, it is possible for us to work in terms of atomic reality. Alone in the room with your ambiguous object and six months time ahead of you, it would have been quite possible for you to call for atomic assessment apparatus and reading material as you proceeded with your study. Those who did not have that word, and thus that construct, could not have pursued such a path in their thinking. Eventually someone might have moved in that direction perhaps, once she or he had produced supporting sets of names (ideas). However, it is unlikely that an atomic reality could exist during the six month period for any of those who had not entered the experience with language capable of developing this way of knowing the world. Harley Shands (1971) wrote that "With words, human beings undertake the conquest of nature—but at the total price of first having unconsciously submitted (long ago in the unrememberable past) to the forcible occupation of the self by the linguistic system into which we happen to have been born" (p. 20). Shands thinks of "naming as a process of stopping movement" (p. 31). Our ways of naming things seduce us into assuming that what we name is static. Western languages, in particular, focus on objects, and we assume objects to be relatively permanent. Vygotsky (1962) is among those who noted that developmentally, languages in their infant stages have tended to emphasize function. Less developed languages rely more heavily on verbs than nouns. It is almost as if our language takes on a life of its own as it grows older. Actually, the language does take on life. It modifies the reality that surrounds us and presents it to us as if it were objective, as if language were delivering to us the pure form of the thing. Originally, in the developing life of a language, the forms apprehended and delivered up to us tended to be moving forms. Our earliest forms of language viewed life in terms of action. When more sophisticated languages were available for transaction with life around us, they began to present us with more concrete rather than fluid realities. Thus, we tend to see permanence rather than change and we tend to assume that stability represents the reality of things.

Shands takes on the question of the possibility of thought without language by commenting that the issue seems to him to be similar to the old issue of whether a tree that falls in the forest makes a noise. That timeworn issue can, of course, never be resolved experientially. We can only reason toward a conclusion. Shands (1971) cannot think a thought without using language to think it. He believes that, "For a thought to 'exist' *incommunicado* is tantamount to nonexistence" (p. 49).

Thus, words and constructs are arguably inseparable. Occasionally, we have a sense of something that we cannot quite put into words. Some might say that this represents an occasion when a thought arrives independent of language. Shands and most of the fifth grade English teachers we have known and loved would not agree. How many times have we all been told that if we cannot talk about it, if we can't write it down, we don't really understand it at all—and isn't this the truth in some important way? During those moments when a thought is tickling at the edges of our understanding, we are quite possibly experiencing a moment when our culture or our individual experiences have not equipped us with the proper language to make the new idea become real for us. It is not that our knowings during these moments are invalid. Rather, we have no way to bring them into actuality for ourselves. Without language, we human beings are really quite lost in the world. Our knowledge of life is a symbolic knowledge. Unlike most of the animal kingdom, we are not forced to deal with life only on a sensory, experiential basis. We use the language given us—and created by us—to slice the world into parts; and these parts become reality. So often, we Westerners think of the reality we create as an objective reality. We have historically neglected to take into account our own contributions to it. We have overlooked our *method* of understanding, the application of language-based constructs to that which we find before us.

And so it is that a tree is really only a tree for you and me. We assume that it is the same tree for all sentient beings; a tree and nothing but a tree. However, the subatomic scientist gazing in the same direction might be much more concerned with a large group of atoms held together in describable ways with most of the area involved containing what could be thought of as space rather than matter. Electrons whirl around nuclei; all is in motion; most of the area is not solid in any conventional sense of that term. A pity, perhaps, that our scientist is not more concerned with the beautiful autumn-colored leaves. Or, perhaps the greater pity is that you and I have little familiarity with the terrain within the subatomic world. But imagine with me an even stranger situation involving a being from another planet that is very different from you and me; perhaps a much larger form containing less "matter." Imagine an intelligent being who is only equipped to apprehend (through its quite different sensory equipment) what is to us very large stretches of things. Perhaps this being only apprehends a forest but never a tree. Maybe our tree appears in this other reality as something analogous to an atom in our world. It is even possible, of course, that trees make very fine food for a jolly green giant-type spaceperson. (Perhaps they disappear in two bites like a stick of broccoli.) The possibilities seem infinite and the conclusion inescapable—we call them the way we see them and we see them through the filter of language. We name as we know; we know as we name. One being's tree is another's food or another's atomic reality. This way of considering the issue brings us squarely into the midst of the epistemological issue. But, before we consider epistemology, it is important that we draw some conclusions for systemic thinking from this discussion of language.

Language: Systemic Suggestions

Systemic perspectives look upon language as the major tool that human beings use for making sense out of the world. Thus, it is given very substantial attention. We must become aware that Western language is a manufactured thing. The words we use do not reflect fundamental or objective reality. They represent ways of relating to life that our forebears found useful. Any word reflects culture every bit as much as it reflects nature. Anyone who attempts to use systemic ways of working with problems needs to give some serious and deliberate thought to the language. We need to become familiar with its characteristic style. There are an infinite number of points of view that Western languages exclude. We can begin to develop an appreciation for this situation as other languages are learned. The further removed from Western thinking, the more a new language presents us with new ways of thinking about the world. The classic oriental phrase, *tao de ching*, represents a way of thinking about life that has been historically fundamental in the East. The phrase refers to a way of life—to *the* way of life to an Eastern mind. It refers to a flow, a rhythmicity that is part of all things. The phrase suggests harmony; it calls for a going with. After presenting 40 words or so in translation of the concept of the *tao*, I find myself on the one hand feeling a bit pleased for having produced a creditable definition of a pretty tricky concept. Yet, on the other hand, I know I do not really grasp the subtleties of the idea of *tao* at all. I haven't spent enough time with Eastern languages; I haven't spent enough time with this very basic idea. Functionally, at this point it is probably true that the idea of *tao de ching* cannot be adequately translated into Western languages. Isn't it astonishing that a premier concept for half the planet is difficult to translate into the languages used by the other half? Doesn't that tell us a great deal about the primacy of language for thought?

Several of the descriptors of systemic thought that will be presented represent characteristic ways of thinking for Western people. Our languages are full of words that can be pressed into service in order to support, explain, and elaborate these ideas. Importantly, most of the issues that will be raised demand consideration because Western languages have emphasized these concepts so much that we take for granted that the words reflect the true nature of things. A systemic perspective requires an assumption that our words reflect ideas and that our ideas are no more than that. They are ideas; they are not reality. They simply give us a way of thinking about the world around us. At this stage in the development of this new way of thinking about the world probably the best and the least we can do is to continually remind ourselves to develop a healthy mistrust of language—at least as a conveyor of absolute truth and objective reality.

EPISTEMOLOGY

As we have seen when considering writers as apparently divergent as Fritjof Capra and John Dewey, epistemology is the most important issue for our consideration. While language is the most basic tool used for understanding, epistemology is the issue in greatest need of understanding, if we are to make a systems shift in our thinking. As defined in Chapter 5, epistemology is concerned with assumptions about how knowing occurs, the rules governing it, and its limits. All people who use language have such a set of assumptions. Classification of the varieties of epistemological belief has traditionally been within the province of philosophy, where the issue has been notorious for its complexity and ability to stimulate controversy. Within this century and especially during the past 25 years, discoveries in the physical sciences have excited broad interest in the idea of epistemology. For many, a thoughtful consideration of the function of human epistemologies has fundamentally changed the way they think about the world.

As early as the 17th and 18th centuries, occasional major thinkers, such as Hume and Kant, helped Western people begin to move away from what has been called *naive realism*. This epistemological point of view was our earliest point of view, at least in the West. Assumptions of naive realism hold that what you see, hear, touch and so forth is the real thing (in itself). There is a one-to-one correspondence between what is out there and your understanding of it. If you see, touch, and smell "tree," then a tree it is; and nothing but a tree—positively, objectively, and really. As other epistemologies began to develop, first in philosophy then in the sciences, many began to change their minds. They did not change their minds about whether the tree was *there*, or whether "tree" provided an accurate description of the thing. Rather, they began to change their minds about the "positively, objectively, and really" part. The change came as a result of learning new ways of thinking about how we come to know anything at all. Developments in modern physics especially (most growing out of issues surrounding the Heisenberg Principle of Uncertainty) have found us reconsidering the age-old belief that it is possible for us to know the one, true essence of a thing. We have become very impressed with the limitations on observation forced upon us by our very own sensory equipment and nervous systems, as well as personal and group cultures.

Lincoln and Guba (1985) put the issue a little more mundanely as they remind us of one sportsperson's *experience* of this "truth." Jocko Conlan, a National League baseball umpire who was trying to describe the standards that make a strike a strike (and a ball a ball) once declared that, "They ain't nothin' till I call 'em."

We have realized that, in order to observe anything, there has to be a somebody to do the observing. And, each and every somebody has a particular frame of reference: a particular language, culture, location in time and space, and so on. All of these things have a tremendous influence on the descriptions that result from observation. Objectivity becomes impossible. Even devices such as one-way mirrors, tape recorders, and television monitors do not prevent us from "disturbing" in a very real sense that which we want to observe in its purest form. For after all, it is we who invent the recorders and stand behind the mirrors. Ultimately, we apply language to what we observe or record for observation later; and *as soon as language is involved, a particular point of view is involved.* The pure essence of the thing is no longer present. Systemic epistemology holds, then, that the only reality we can know is the reality born of the inevitable transaction between the observer and the observed, the knower and that which is known.

Epistemology: Systemic Suggestions

Some inescapable conclusions flow from the epistemological point of view that finds the only knowable reality to be that which is formed when the observer comes into contact with the observed. Lack of access to the "real" essence of things creates some special problems for human beings, which are creatures who have among other things distinguished themselves by a passion for understanding the world and for trying to know it. We can see that the problems are compounded geometrically when we consider that this idea runs counter to conventional wisdom. For centuries, the average Western person believed that it was possible to know things as they "really" are. Thus, in mid-20th century, we find ourselves in the strange position of being victims of our past construal of the situation. We have to unlearn our naively realistic points of view. There are several important places to start. For example, it is crucial that we take a fresh look at issues such as validity and relativity as we design intervention strategies that are basically systemic.

Within this perspective, a traditional notion of validity becomes impossible to sustain. The conventional definition asserts that something is valid if it corresponds to the facts. We think of something as valid if it reflects the "truth" of the matter. Thus, the idea of validity has carried with it the assumption that *the* truth can be known. We judge the validity of our ideas in terms of the extent to which they correspond to an objective truth.

If one assumes that objective reality cannot be known in its most pure form, what happens to the idea of validity? Can anything ever be valid? The answer is decidedly yes. However, the interpretation of the validity construct changes. Within systemic thinking, the only standard for the validity of things must be some sort of agreement. If we can never learn the true essence of what we seek to understand, then the best we can achieve in terms of validity is an interjudge reliability. Something is valid to the extent that people agree that it is so. Consensual validation becomes the only possible form of validation.

This is a pragmatic position. If we cannot know an objective reality, then it becomes practical to proceed on the basis of what the most informed persons, or the majority, believe to be the case. For example, when a health-related diagnosis is unavailable concerning the cause of a patient's recent sluggishness, the version of reality provided by physicians that the patient respects will probably be believed. This is not necessarily a majority opinion; rather, it is believed to be an informed opinion. In other cases, we have a history of believing that only the majority opinion will do. Chairs are for sitting on, for example. A couple of the world's most eminent furniture design experts cannot tell us that tables are for sitting on and chairs are for sleeping in.

While this way of thinking about validity seems strange at first glance, systemic theorists believe that this is the way we have always operated. We just haven't been aware of it. Our access to the truth has always been limited. It is possible that an absolute standard for things exists, we just cannot get to it. We always find ourselves in the way. Even the incredibly crucial issue of knowledge concerning the existence and nature of God has always been dependent on one's position in space and time. Despite the variety of beliefs concerning God across ages and cultures, each person has always assumed that his or her group possesses the truth. I reason that if most everybody I know and trust believes it, then it must be true. The generations before me also reasoned this way. Practically, agreement has always constituted the most powerful criterion for validity among human beings. Considered this way, the issue of the relative nature of truth takes on a new dimension. The relativity of things is not so exclusively a matter for concern within science as it is an accepted fact of everyday existence.

When adopting a systemic perspective, then, it is important to realize that an objective reality is not available to us. Because of this basic idea, we can enjoy the freedom of taking another look at our most fundamental beliefs as Western scientists and practitioners. The remaining ideas included in this chapter represent perspectives that are peculiarly Western and no longer constitute a useful way of looking at things, if we are to move in new directions armed with some of the exciting new developments coming out of the sciences these days. If we are to get hold of the newer systemic ways of thinking, we must begin by appreciating the limitations imposed by our languages and epistemologies. A recognition of these limitations finds us in a position to reinterpret such basic Western notions as linearity, causality, and so forth. Each of these constructs demands attention as we reform our world view.

LINEARITY AND NONLINEARITY: RECURSION

Webster's *New World Dictionary* (1980) offers over 100 lines of definition for the term *line* and its associates such as linear and lineal. The term *nonlinear*, however, is not defined at all. It can be found within a lengthy list of terms containing the prefix *non-*. This list is introduced as one which, "includes the more common compounds formed with non- that do not have special meanings; they will be understood if *not* is used before the meaning of the base word." Thus, Webster's provides dramatic evidence that the

American version of Western thinking is heavily invested in the concept of linearity while *nonlinearity* is a term considered to have no "special meanings." There are a multitude of ways to think about lines in the English language, most of them are dependent upon ideas of length, extension, and directness. Nonlinearity is thought of simply as being not related to lines. Nonlinearity is, thus, defined in terms of what it is not, in terms of its opposite. In contrast, opposites such as *up* and *down* are very different words with clearly defined meanings. Nonetheless, they anchor a bipolar construct in the same way that linear and nonlinear are apparently intended to do. The major difference is that the term *nonlinearity* is an empty category. It is an idea that is little-used in this language; thus, there are very few words that convey its meaning. Later in this discussion, the term *recursion* is nominated as the most useful for representing the opposite of linearity. First, however, it is important to think about the traditional meanings of linearity and the traditional confusions associated with attempts to understand its opposite.

Anthropologist Dorothy Lee inspected uses of the terms *lineal* and *nonlineal* from a cross-cultural perspective. Her conclusions support the Whorfian hypothesis that people are not led by the same picture of the universe if their languages are not equivalent. A Lee article (1950), *Codifications of reality: Lineal and nonlineal*, contrasts the Western assumption of a linear world with the nonlinear world view of the Trobriand Islands. She makes the point that Trobriand language does not provide for temporal or spatial linear connections between objects. Circularity is considered by Lee to be a specific form of linearity since a circle is formed by a bent line. She finds a striking example of what we are talking about in Malinowski's description of the islands. Lee (1950/1973, pp. 133-134) writes

> But is the line present in reality? Malinowski, writing for members of our culture and using idiom which could be comprehensible to them, described the Trobriand Village as follows: "Concentrically with the circular row of yam houses there runs a ring of dwelling huts." He saw, or at any rate, he represented the village as two circles. But in the texts which he recorded we find that the Trobrianders at no time mention circles or rings or even rows when they refer to their villages. Any word which they use to refer to a village, such as *a* or *this*, is prefixed by the substantive element *kway* which means *bump* or *aggregate of bumps*. This is the element which they use when they refer to a pimple or a bulky rash or to canoes loaded with yams. In their terms, a village is an aggregate of bumps; are they blind to the circles? Or did Malinowski create the circles himself, out of his cultural axioms?

At this point the concept of nonlinearity may be as difficult for the Western mind as is the linear assumption for the Trobriand mind. We think of such basic ideas as time, space, and growth in terms of our linear assumption. Time marches forward or back; we expect our children to grow up straight and our rows of corn to stand tall. In fact, most of the basic concepts we use to make sense out of the universe are dependent upon the idea of linearity. A linear way of construing reality is so ingrained within our culture that we can scarcely imagine that another way of dealing with our surroundings might be possible. Even as systemic thinkers attempt to break away from dependency upon the linear construct, many find themselves simply moving toward substitution of ideas of circularity — a concept which is clearly contained within the fundamental idea of the line. A circle is a bent line that connects with itself.

For the most part, the nonlinearity construct is truly an empty category within our Western mode of thought. We have fuzzy notions about it and our language is inadequate for the development of the idea at this point. The mainstream epistemologies and languages to which we are heir make it impossible for us to have an adequate understanding of what the opposite of linearity might be. Thus, it is at this point that we are brought up short in our attempts to construct an alternate world view that contains concepts that are fresh to the Western mind. Systemic writers struggle mightily with this problem but, unfortunately, fail as often as succeed. While some of the other new ideas found in this chapter represent language categories that are fuller than they used to be, the idea of nonlinearity lags behind developmentally. What is the alternative to construing the world in terms of straight lines (or crooked lines, broken lines, circles, or meanders, for that matter)? And what are the typical styles of thinking which support this world view?

Forty years ago, as Dewey and Bentley were struggling to present a transactional viewpoint to the social sciences, they noted their habit of speaking of "this" as being equivalent to "that." Using our current systems terminology, we would say that they were talking about the need to consider patterns and redundancies, to abandon reliance on linear logic. Dewey and Bentley, however, had even fewer language tools available to them than we do. They tended to hyphenate phrases in order to communicate their rejection of traditional language as adequate for description from a transactional view. In attempting to describe what we now think of as nonlinearity, they wrote that

> When we said above that designations are events and events designations, we adopted *circularity* — procedure in a circle — openly, explicitly, emphatically. . . . We have nothing to apologize for in the circularity we choose in preference to the old talk-ways. We observe world-being-known-to-man-in-it; we report the observation; we proceed to inquire into it, circularity or no circularity. This is all there is to it. And the circularity is not merely round the circle in one direction; the course is both ways round at once in full mutual function. (Dewey & Bentley, 1949, p. 109)

In trying to define a concept that is opposite to the linear construct they relied on the word, *circularity* — an unfortunate choice because the term can refer to a special case of linearity. Some of the thinking in the paragraph just cited gives a feel for what we are beginning to understand as nonlinearity. As Dewey and Bentley write that "the course is both ways round at once in full mutual function," we can see that they were conceptually headed in the direction of contemporary systemic thinkers, who think about feedback, mutuality, recursiveness, and the qualitative as they attempt to get hold of this will-o-the-wisp idea.

Some of the systemic writers continue to rely on the term *circularity* as they describe the opposite of linearity. While it is functional to depend on a term that is very different from the word *linearity* as we define the opposite end of this presumed continuum, the word *circular* is an unfortunate choice. Nevertheless, it will be important eventually to stick fast to a term that is as different from linearity as is the term night with reference to day or short with reference to tall. Shands (1971) comments on the developmental progression of opposites in language by noting that our first task is "separating 'A' from 'Not A' and then taking 'Not A' to a new naming as 'B' and separating 'B' from 'Not B' " (p. 46). Although we are developmentally ready for "B" in the case under discussion here, the designation *circularity* does not work well because it allows too much dependence on the linear notion. Hoffman (1981) has written that

> The central concept of the new epistemology—both the homeostatic and the evolutionary paradigms—is the idea of circularity. In the field of mental health there has been a growing disenchantment with the linear causality of Western thought. Mental illness has traditionally been thought of in linear terms, with historical, causal explanations for the distress. . . . After decades of strict adherence to these models, a new conceptualization began to emerge. Evidence provided by the watchers behind the screen supported the growing disenchantment with the linear, historical view. If one saw a person with a psychiatric affliction in a clinician's office, it would be easy to assume that he or she suffered from an intrapsychic disorder arising from the past. But if one saw the same person with his or her family, in the context of current relationships, one began to see something quite different. One would see communications and behaviors from everybody present, composing many circular causal loops that played back and forth, with the behavior of the afflicted person only part of a larger recursive dance. (pp. 4–7)

Hoffman is one of those who depends on the word *circularity* to convey the meaning of nonlinearity. This practice, however, can confuse us at times because it is easy to let our conventional understanding of the term get in the way.

The Milan Associates lamented the heavy dependence we have on linear ways of thinking and focused on linear causality as a particularly disadvantageous concept when working within a systemic framework. Following the lead of Bateson, they see that our language, especially "the verb, *to be* condemns us to think according to the linear model, to make arbitrary punctuation, to inquire on the reality of undecidables, and to postulate that a causality exists, thus losing ourselves in an intricacy of endless explanations and hypotheses" (Selvini-Palozzoli, Cecchin, Prata, & Boscolo, 1978, p. 27). Without providing a detailed explanation of their understanding of the linear and nonlinear concepts they, nonetheless, offer the reader suggestions for viable language alternatives for the verb *to be*. The verb *to show* reduces the impact of a linear world view when used in place of *to be*. The following excerpt from one of their family sessions illustrates the point:

> The father, Mr. Franchi, shows, during the session, a veiled erotic interest in the designated patient, who, for her part, shows hostility and scorn toward him. Mrs. Franchi shows an intense jealousy toward husband and daughter, while she shows a strong affection toward her other daughter, who in turn, shows no sign of reciprocating this affection. (Selvini-Palazzoli et al., 1978, p. 28)

Keeney* has acknowledged that he prefers the term *lineal* over linear, as a result of his intention to follow the lead of Bateson in this matter. Bateson defined the terms in the following way:

> Linear is a technical term in mathematics describing a relationship between variables such that when they are plotted against each other on orthogonal Cartesian coordinates, the result will be a straight line. Lineal describes a relation among a series of causes or arguments such that the sequence does not come back to the starting point. The opposite of linear is nonlinear. The opposite of lineal is recursive. (Keeney, 1983, p. 228)

Standard English usage dictionaries do not make this distinction. Bateson's argument here is a technical one. Rather than merely reporting lexicographic information, he is creating it. In an important way for systemic psychology, his distinction is unnecessary and perhaps misleading. If he reserves the term *linear* for the field of geometry, he must conclude that its opposite can be represented by the term *nonlinear*, a term that we have seen contains no special meaning. If he relies on lineal, he is bound by a little

---

*Keeney (1983) draws specific attention to the nonlinear construct only as he draws a distinction between lineal and nonlineal epistemology. He notes that nonlineal also has been "called systemic, ecological, ecosystemic, circular, recursive, or cybernetic" (p. 14). He says that "nonlineal epistemology emphasizes ecology, relationship, and whole systems" (p. 14). Clearly, there is a confusion here. Some of the terms are appropriate to the idea of epistemology, while others might be more specifically related to the idea of nonlinearity. The two words, *nonlineal* and *epistemology*, are not only complementary, but they are also not clearly understood at this point in our everyday language and cultural development. Thus, it is not very helpful to combine them until an adequate definition of each has been provided. Those who have been struggling with these ideas for some time will understand Keeney at this point in his writing; others may find the issue to be more muddied than elucidated.

used but conventional definition, which seriously limits the idea he is trying to convey.

It seems appropriate, for practical reasons, to use the term *linear*, since it captures the essence of what we are talking about and is the more common of the two length-oriented terms. It is probably for this latter reason that it is used so much more often by systemic writers than is the word *lineal*.

Recursive

Bateson's identification of the term recursive as opposite to lineal provides us with an excellent starting point as we begin to create a definition of what the nonlinear idea is all about. Once again, dictionary sources tend to be unhelpful. A survey of the latest editions of the four major American language dictionaries revealed that none of them contained the terms *recursion* or *recursive*. Webster's *Third New International Dictionary* (1981) provides a mathematical definition, which considers recursive to reflect a function whereby the nth case can be defined in terms of the previous steps.* This notion is not uncomplementary with the way the word is currently being used in systemic psychology; however, it is too mathematically technical to be of much use.

Recursive is a good choice for a term that captures the essence of nonlinearity and, thus, stands as the opposite of linear. While the term is used often in the systemic literature, it is rarely defined independent of other constructs that seem to be at issue for the writers. Therefore, we give it more attention here than will eventually be necessary, once progressively larger numbers of people become familiar with systems-oriented ideas and begin to apply them across a variety of fields. Undoubtedly, the term *recursive* will be found in years to come in common usage dictionaries outside the specialized systems fields, where it is now relatively prevalent.

A recursive phenomenon is the product of multidirectional feedback, which occurs as functional and arbitrarily identifiable parts of a system engage in transaction across time and space. A recursion is nonlinear; there is mutuality of influence. Any event that can be identified within a recursive human network can be viewed as the product of experience and anticipation. That is, any isolated movement or moment can be seen to be influenced by events in the past, present, and future. The path of power is a mutual path.

For example, the flow of the dynamics in a family system can be viewed

---

*For an interesting discussion of some of the confusions and uses of the terms *recursion* and *recursive*, the reader is referred to Hofstadter (1980). Across some disciplines, one of these related terms can have opposite meanings in some contexts.

as recursive, not linear, when we see that the family members mutually influence one another's thinking and behavior. Any family event contains stored information within each person about past events; there is a set of attitudes about present conditions that exist and are important; and anticipations play an influential role as the actors and actresses imagine the future course of things. As I began to talk here about a family event, I presented it to you in terms of past, present, and future, a linear construction, because I am aware that such a way of viewing must be acknowledged. It is our conventional way and we are forced to use it, even as we attempt to move out of it. What I am hoping to convey, however, is that within a systems framework, past, present, and future inform the present moment in a recursive fashion. It is not important, systemically, to identify the relative contributions of each; in fact, to do so would be to re-enter our linear, Western ways of construing reality. Therefore, when a son shows his anger in the presence of parents and siblings, who evidence silent scorn, it is not helpful from a systemic perspective to trace linear paths of causality onto the scene. It is more useful within this perspective to think of mutuality of influence and feedback loops. For example, we might say that within this family, a recurrent pattern involves the coexistence of anger and silence. Anger might ripple from family member to family member but as it does so, the rest of the system falls habitually silent. This way of regarding the situation finds us asking a different kind of post-observational question, such as "What is the function of this pattern? How does it serve the family?"

Although he relies on the term *circular* in a complementary line of thought, Shands thinks of behaving as a recursive phenomenon and describing as a linear phenomenon. A cognitive behavior or movement is not a linear experience. It is only as we attempt to describe it — to become aware of what we have experienced — that we Westerners see the experience as linear. As we thought about Aunt Minerva's annual holiday dinner in a previous chapter, the natural tendency was to describe in terms of cause-effect sequences. However, the actual experience of the food, the laughter, or the stress was one of immediacy and mutuality. Instantaneous feedback was a distinguishing feature of the moment. Just exactly where the feedback came from (within? without? her, him, me?) is not relevant to this type of behavioral understanding. A recursive reality does not contain linear components and is not to be interpreted from a linear point of view.* As we muddle toward an understanding of this once-empty category of nonlinearity, it is

---

*Occasionally, a connection becomes apparent between the idea of recursion and Carl Jung's notion of synchronicity. Jung thought of synchronous events as those which contained lateral associations and connections. While his epistomology is a bit positivist on this point, it is possibly fair to think of synchronicity as a special case of describing reality in which linear causation is not present.

important to remind ourselves that an "objective" reality is not necessarily recursive nor is it linear in its absolute essence. These are merely two ways of viewing reality. They are epistemological devices.

At this point, let us return to Bateson's thinking on this issue. With reasoning similar to that of Bertrand Russell (1960), Bateson thinks of the verbs *to be* and *to have* as the major contributors to linear thinking in the Western languages. He notes that we typically speak of things as having certain qualities and being a certain way. The desk before me is wood, brown, small, heavy, and so forth. Things are and have characteristics. He points out that this way of talking is "satisfactory for everyday living." We say that "This computer is portable." "That boy has acne." "The cabbage heads are huge." "The price is too high." While such statements comprise useful everyday language, Bateson believes that

> This way of talking is not good enough in science or epistemology. To think straight, it is advisable to expect all qualities and attributes, adjectives, and so on to refer to at least *two* sets of interactions in time. "The stone is hard" means (a) that when poked it resisted penetration and (b) that certain continual interactions among the molecular *parts* of the stone in some way bond the parts together.
> "The stone is stationary" comments on the location of the stone relative to the location of the speaker and other possible moving things. It also comments on matters internal to the stone: its inertia, lack of internal distortion, lack of friction at the surface, and so on. Language continually asserts by the syntax of subject and predicate that "things" somehow "have qualities and attributes." A more precise way of talking would insist that the "things" are produced, are seen as separate from other "things," are made "real" by their internal relations and by their behavior in relationship with other things and with the speaker. (1979, p. 61)

Once again, Bateson has pointed the way. While the concept of recursion is misty at the moment, it is possible to begin to work with it effectively if we can eliminate those language components which strengthen a linear picture of our lives. As mentioned earlier, Selvini-Palazzoli and her associates opted for such an approach and have been notably successful with it.

Linearity and Recursion: Systemic Suggestions

In order to shift to a systemic perspective, one must first adopt an epistemological position that affirms linearity as a convenient and typically Western way of looking at things rather than a reflection of an absolute reality. Once such a supposition begins to be a useful one, the challenge of creating strategies for forcing ourselves away from linear views and toward recursive thinking looms large.

A good place to begin is with the language. The verbs *to be* and *to have* lock us into looking at things in terms of straight lines. They force us to isolate a part of a living system and then to treat it as if it were an independent whole, which exclusively possesses characteristics and is the sole owner of behaviors. Thus, much can be accomplished in service of the development of recursive constructs simply by eliminating our impressive dependence on these verbs. Much of the time this task is easier said than done. The usefulness of a team approach to systemic psychology cannot be stressed enough. For many of us, constant reminders concerning language finally starts to do the trick. We begin to change our patterns of speech, and thus our habits of thought.

Several groups of verbs provide viable substitutions for *to be* and *to have*. What can be thought of as the *to show* group contains verbs which can easily replace *is* in descriptions of interpersonal dynamics. Included in this group are *show, tell, reveal, display, demonstrate, make known, exhibit, indicate, evidence*, and *manifest*. Instead of observing that "She is forceful; He is hurt; They are confused; She is angry," and so forth, observation that includes other verbs can permit the recursive aspects of an event to be revealed. Different pictures are revealed as we observe that, "She manifests forcefulness; He displays hurt; They tell of confusion; She demonstrates anger."

A second group of verbs provides useful alternatives to the linear notion of possession, which is found in expressions such as "He has lots of poise in difficult situations; He has a lot of bottled up anger inside; She hasn't got a clue about what is going on in that situation." This second set can be thought of as the *to stand for* group. It contains such verbs as *suggest, designate, signify, represent, specify, symbolize*, and *express*. Use of these terms results in observations like "He stands for poise in difficult situations; He symbolizes bottled up anger; She represents innocence in that situation."

Avoiding the linearity contained in directly causal statements sometimes can occur when the verb *to relate* and some of its associates are employed. "Her timidity causes the mother to become violent" can be eliminated with an observation such as "Timidity and violence are often associated within the relationship of these women." This group contains such constructs as *associate, connect, co-occur, cohere, communicate, join*, and *juxtapose*. "Severe dieting causes binging then guilt" becomes expressed as "The coherence of dieting, binging, and guilt is a dynamic that satisfies an important family stability need." "Frustration breeds aggression" becomes "Frustration joins aggression as phases of action that fulfill communication needs within this classroom group."

While it is possible to reconstrue causal statements in this way, it is probably unwise to rely on this strategy, since it forces us to find a rather stressful balance between the older linear ways of thinking and the newer recursive ways. Causality is so deeply ingrained in us that an attempt to reframe causal statements into relational statements usually finds us continuing to rely on the notion of temporal sequence, even though such reliance is often subtle. Identification of the causal phenomenon in terms of a whole, rather than components, followed by a statement of the function of the dynamic for the system of interest constitutes an approach less fraught with danger. For example, given the frustration-causes-aggression situation, a systemic view might look for, "quick bursts of acting out which serve as necessary tools for maintenance of an important family dynamic (such as reconnecting after periods of silent distance or other types of emotional distance)."

It is often possible to interchange verbs from one group or another. As we get more sophisticated with respect to the concept of recursion, we will learn more specific expressions that we will come to think of as perfectly suited to specific observations. It is very possible that the sets just identified might be collapsed into one group. However, it has proven useful for me to think of *to show*, *to stand for*, and *to relate* as three sets of ideas, which provide an arsenal of opportunity for changing the language to reflect more recursive ways of observing what is before us.

CAUSALITY

Many of the comments about linearity, language, and epistemology also apply to causality. Within the epistemological point of view supported here, describing events in causal terms is considered only one way of construing things. The identification of causation serves a practical function for the conduct of daily living and within many spheres of scientific reference as well. Viewing things in such a way as to ascribe causality is very helpful within a Newtonian world view. However, when one takes a look at the world, it is not absolutely necessary to see causality. There are other ways of observing and naming events. Systemic theory suggests that the Western world's dependence on the causal construct is maladaptive when trying to observe wholes and to understand organic systems.

When we break a natural unity into parts, we use causality to hook them back together again. For example, if we take a marriage and break it into husband and wife, the concept of causality is used repeatedly as we deal with the relation between them. She causes him to do this; he causes her to do that. Such a way of construing reality yields much practical information and in many cases provides a rich understanding of the events of interest. Viewing a whole rather than breaking it into parts also yields productive information.

The important issue here is not whether causality actually exists in the world. Rather, the issue becomes one of deciding when it is helpful to take a causal view and when it is fruitful to adopt another perspective. Causality is important in a mechanical realm but doesn't quite work with organic phenomena. Machines are structured; their parts are balanced in causal interdependence. A key causes the ignition to activate, which causes the battery to boot up the pistons, which start other engine processes, and the results can be seen all over America each morning at 7:45. However, living systems are not machines. They are processes rather than structures. Capra talks about the need to bring the mechanical view and the organic view into greater balance than has previously been the case. He comments that:

> Machines function according to linear chains of cause and effect, and when they break down a single cause for the breakdown can usually be identified. In contrast, the functioning of organisms is guided by cyclical patterns of information flow known as feedback loops. For example, component A may affect component B; B may affect C; and C may "feed back" the influence to A and thus close the loop. When such a system breaks down, the breakdown is usually caused by multiple factors that may amplify each other through interdependent feedback loops. Which of these factors was the initial cause of the breakdown is often irrelevant.
>
> This nonlinear interconnectedness of living organisms indicates that the conventional attempts of biomedical science to associate diseases with single causes are highly problematic. . . . The systems view makes it clear that genes do not uniquely determine the functioning of an organism as cogs and wheels determine the working of a clock. Rather, genes are integral parts of an ordered whole and thus conform to its systemic organization. (Capra, 1982, p. 269)

Elsewhere, as Capra describes the vast differences between phenomena at the macro and micro levels, he reminds us of the well-known statement of James Jeans, "that the stream of knowledge is heading towards a nonmechanical reality; the universe begins to look more like a great thought than like a great machine." That statement implies more of a positivist point of view than a systemic theorist is compelled to take. That is, it suggests that the universe *is* a particular way (really, truly, absolutely). The point of view espoused here does not require absolutes. Rather, it encourages us to consider that moving away from nonmechanical construals of reality is probably a very useful move to make right now. Abandoning causal models will allow us to see a newer reality that will help us to make a different way in the world — under some circumstances, undoubtedly a better way.

When describing the remarkably different behavior of subatomic phenomena, Capra writes

> This does not mean that atomic events occur in completely arbitrary fashion; it means only that they are not brought about by local causes. The behavior of any part is determined by its nonlocal connections to the whole, and since we do not know these connections precisely, we have to replace the narrow classical notion of cause and effect by the wider concept of statistical causality. The laws of atomic physics are statistical laws, according to which the probabilities for atomic events are determined by the dynamics of the whole system. Whereas in classical mechanics the properties and behavior of the parts determine those of the whole, the situation is reversed in quantum mechanics: it is the whole that determines the behavior of the parts. (Capra, 1982, p. 86)

As noted over and over again by the writers considered here, causality is not an important concept when working within a systemic model. In fact, it is important to discard the idea of causality. Elimination of causal thinking is a necessity when working systemically with families, classrooms, schools, and other unities. When we wish to relate the family or classroom to *another* system, causality is necessary. So often, the causal notion provides the bridge between two entities. When we try to understand a whole and our involvement in that whole, however, causality prevents us from doing so, because it is a concept that cannot function without parts. As soon as we apply causal thinking, we must see parts, not a whole. Something must do something to a *separate* something. A whole cannot be viewed as acting upon itself. Even when we observe a dog chasing its tail, we separate the tail from the dog. We see the teeth that bite the tail; we see parts. At all times, when we think of a person or animal acting upon itself we think of it in terms of the parts of that person or animal acting on other parts. Clearly, reliance on causality must be suspended if we are to begin to understand living systems as systems, as organic wholes.

Acausality is the term sometimes used to refer to the opposite of causality. Like nonlinearity, acausality is currently an empty category in our language. Only occasionally do we find a dictionary that defines the term, and it is always defined in terms of its opposite. Unlike the idea of nonlinearity, however, it is not necessary for systemic purposes that we develop a clearer definition of acausality. When working in this particular systems model, we simply drop the causality concept.

Acausality: Systemic Suggestions

It is important that the stranglehold of the concept of causality on our Western minds be loosened. This is not an easy task to accomplish. Constant reminders are necessary because we leap toward causal thought almost from the moment of awakening each morning. Again, it is helpful to develop a team approach, where each member of the psychological or educational team feels free to give language feedback or to solicit it.

The prime target for change is language. The lists of alternative verbs contained within the discussions of linearity and recursion can be particularly helpful. Developing lists of additional words can provide excellent practice in learning to think through this important issue.

Experimentation with looking at situations and systems as wholes is crucial. I recommend taking the time to observe a living system, such as a pet or young child, in action. Establish a 15-minute block of time and assign yourself the task of simply observing the toddler (or cat or whatever) as a unity. Just watch—and think of the whole. Watch for process and movement and pattern and redundancy and recursiveness. After engaging in this activity on several occasions you will begin to get a feel for the thing — and for the possibilities inherent in this new way of thinking. In addition, you will begin to notice which things act as cues that propel you into causal observation. A rhythm will emerge in which you will eventually be able to move from systemic to causal observation and back again.

Causality provides a way of making sense out of the Newtonian world in which we spend the majority of our day. It allows us to organize sequences of events in a meaningful manner. Acausal ways of viewing have allowed us to discover undreamed of worlds in physics, biology, and family systems. More is undoubtedly yet to come.

FORMS OF REASONING

Aristotle gave the Western world a system of reasoning — deduction — that has hardly been tampered with since its formation during the fourth century B.C. He believed that his form of logical reasoning provided *the* standard for the validity of thought. While we have concluded through the years that there are other right ways of reasoning in addition to Aristotle's, many dictionaries still define logic or deductive reasoning by claiming for it the status of ultimate measure of valid thought. In other words, reasoning is not correct if it does not use legitimate deductive processes. Aristotelian deduction is linear: it moves from the general principle to the specific case. The classic representation of deductive logic is found in the syllogism. The classic syllogism is attributed, of course, to Aristotle, who is believed to have said that

All men are mortal.
Socrates is a man.
Therefore, Socrates is mortal.

We rely on the deductive syllogism countless times each day. For example, consider the following thoughts:

Jim's markets always have produce sales on Saturday.
Today is Saturday.
Therefore, Jim's is having a produce sale.

Everyone who lives in that neighborhood is wealthy.
Bill and Nancy live in that neighborhood.
Therefore, Bill and Nancy are wealthy.

As the age of empiricism burst into 17th and 18th century European affairs, another form of logic captured the imagination of Western humanity. In contrast to the deductive Aristotelian method, it became known as *induction*. Induction is also linear, but the direction can be thought of as up rather than down. This method of reasoning moves from the particular up to the general case. The method was born from the necessity to make sense out of information resulting from observation. Empiricism called for gathering data about specific events and drawing general conclusions from such a collection of observations. Induction provided the needed legitimate process of reasoning to support this kind of human activity. It is a form of reasoning, then, that is closely associated with science — classical or 18th century science. Induction is peculiarly Newtonian in that sense. Contemporary folks use induction constantly when reasoning in ways such as

Each morning I have three cups of coffee before 10 AM.
Each morning at 10:30 I get jittery and ill-tempered.
Three coffees cause late morning jitters and ill-temper.

My daughter plays with your daughter every Saturday.
Every Saturday night my daughter uses foul language.
Playing with your daughter encourages foul language.
(Extension: It's your daughter's fault.)

The basic difference between deductive and inductive reasoning is a difference in direction. Deduction moves from a general principle to a particular instance. Induction moves from a particular instance to a general principle. Both methods are linear. The logical path is a straight path. These methods of reasoning are the most important methods for Western thinkers. Our cultures have resulted from processes of inductive and deductive reasoning.

A third form of reasoning has received increased scholarly attention during the past 40 years or so. In contrast to the two methods described above, this method involves lateral processes of cognition. Conventionally, we have referred to this method as *reasoning by analogy*. Bateson (1979) calls it *abductive reasoning*.

When we reason abductively (by analogy) we use the form, "this is to this as that is to that." Abduction concentrates on pattern similarities and differences. Nashville is to Tennessee as Columbus is to Ohio. In that sentence, the logical pattern supporting the relationship of Nashville to Tennessee has been superimposed on the relationship of Columbus to Ohio. Nashville is a city, an American state capital. Thus, only Columbus can satisfy logical conditions for relationship to Ohio in this abduction, since it is a city and also is the capital of Ohio. Analogical reasoning has been associated primarily with American Indian cultures, African cultures, and some aspects of Eastern reasoning. However, reasoning by analogy is nothing new to human beings of all cultures. Most typical Westerners use abduction pretty consistently as they make their way in the world. Many have noted that creative insights emerge from this kind of reasoning (cf., Oppenheimer, 1956; Shrady, 1972; Torrance, 1961). Typical abductive statements in Western thought sound like:

The fresh fish section at my favorite food store chain is near the fresh meat. While not large, the display case is white and a bit old-fashioned looking; I can reasonably hope to find fresh fish in a similar display case in a similar location in this new store.

Maggie and Augie have in common that they are both psychologists, live on the East Coast, are patient, enjoy gentleness, and appreciate me. They are unalike in that Augie lives downtown in a large city; Maggie lives in a cabin in the mountains. (Conclusion: They are more alike than they are different.)

Other illustrations can be found in proverbs and some colloquial expressions. These sayings are the result of abductive reasoning processes and are used to illustrate similarities and differences. For example:

> Birds of a feather flock together.
> Don't throw pearls before swine.

In the first expression, we mean that just as birds of the same kind group and travel together, so do human beings with similar traits. The second proverb indicates that just as it would be foolish to throw a valuable item such as a pearl in front of a pig (who would not appreciate it), it is unwise to offer your own precious talents and characteristics to people who cannot appreciate them due to their own limitations.

While these three forms of reasoning—deduction, induction, and abduction—certainly do not exhaust the possibilities for productive thinking, they are the types most often used by Western minds. From a tendency to rely heavily on deduction and induction, the abductive form is beginning to receive more attention, as we move out of the 20th century.

Abduction is well suited for use with systemic psychology. Rather than reasoning in directly linear fashion, analogical reasoning is concerned with patterns and relationships. Patterns are mentally superimposed upon one another in order to inspect their goodness of fit. A songwriter who scans the memory for tunes similar to the one just written is reasoning by abduction. The search is for a similar arrangement of notes and timing. Another example can be found in a scientist who (a) understands that in another scientific area, Principle A applies under two or three specific conditions and (b) then wonders whether the complementary situations in his or her scientific area might not also contain a principle that functions in a similar fashion. A third example can be created as we inspect the previous two sentences. An application of our own abductive processes will reveal that the songwriter and scientist are using similar mental strategies. Of course, abductive processes need not always culminate in conclusions that certain patterns are approximately equivalent. Using the abductive approach, we often decide that certain conditions are unalike. It is not the results that distinguish this mode of logic, it is the process—an inspection across sets of relationships.

Abduction: Systemic Suggestions

Further development of our abductive ways of thinking is important as we move into an alternate world view. The deductive and inductive processes are essentially linear. In addition, the inductive method lends itself to a sometimes subtle but easy shift toward attribution. Inductive processes are especially weighted in favor of making causal connections. Within everyday thinking, these causal connections can ease toward blame. Reasoning through use of analogy provides an excellent way of seeing relationships rather than causes, connections rather than faults.

The major way to develop abductive reasoning skills is to practice answering the question: "How are these two (or more) phenomena alike and how are they different?" In order to answer this question, processes of abduction are required. In a classroom, we might ask what characteristics event A shares with event B, even though they seem dissimilar but both contain angry children. In a family, we might be concerned with the commonalities found in situations that also contain the regular use of certain verb forms, such as *don't, stop, and quit*.

Analogical reasoning is balanced. It almost has a nicely aesthetic quality to it. It is probably fair to think of it as aesthetic reasoning since pattern is balanced against pattern in logical relationship. If Jane's anger shows when David's abruptness is present, then which of Jane's possible motivators might be available to her in the same way as David's defensiveness is available? Is it fear? In other words, do defensiveness and abruptness relate to David in a way complementary to the connection of fear and anger with Jane? Are both experience patterns part of a single picture for that couple?

WHOLES

The preceding discussions of language, epistemology, linearity, causality, and logic could not escape consideration of an orientation toward wholes rather than parts. Thus, the case for identifying the system as the unit we should pay attention to has been made already from several different vantage points. Obviously, all varieties of systems theory, including the systemic, orient toward unities. They focus on a system.

In the previous discussions, we noted the importance from this point of view of developing language that designates natural wholes rather than parts; of adopting acausal frameworks that allow the integrity of organic unities to remain intact; of thinking in terms of recursive rather than linear feedback of information and influence within a system. All of these approaches protect the coherence of a system under observation. It is important not to fracture a natural social unity, such as a family or classroom, into artificial parts during the attempt to understand it or to intervene.

Wholes: Systemic Suggestions

Practice in focusing on a system rather than its parts is not always easy. A suggestion was made earlier, during the discussion of causality, that 15-minute observations of a moving child or pet can aid the shift toward seeing unities rather than components. Adopting the same perspective while observing a committee at work, a classroom group, or a family at a dinner table also can help quite a bit. The goal is simply to see the one rather than the many.

An additional strategy involves identifying a specific relationship, such as a marriage, and observing it in action for a specified period of time with the purpose of describing patterns of movement: verbal or nonverbal, or both. Remember, you are watching a *marriage*, not a husband and wife. You are observing a relationship. This can be a very challenging task, especially for the beginner. However, it yields much useful information and helps us begin to see something in its organic wholeness. Use of this strategy finds us describing in different ways. Instead of noting that "when she does this, he does that," we begin to describe processes that are descriptive of the whole. For example, we see relief or confusion or fear. This kind of perspective is invaluable for systemic descriptions or interventions. Usually, a systemic observation of wholeness results in descriptions of patterns — perhaps the pattern of fear as it ripples through the whole, swelling with silence then subsiding during argument, then swelling out of silence once again.

PATTERNS AND RULES

A pattern is an identifiable arrangement of relationships. It can be a theme or a form. Patterns have recognizable gestalts; that is, the arrangement of relationships within a pattern produces an organization that is experienced as a whole. One of the definitions contained in *Webster's New World Dictionary* (1980) identifies a pattern as, "a regular, mainly unvarying way of acting or doing." This idea is complementary with the idea of a "rule of behavior."

Rules are patterns of behavior that are formally or informally prescribed. They are codes or customs. Rules regulate the pattern of relationships within human systems, such as families, clubs, schools, cities, and so forth.

The idea of rule and the idea of pattern are similar but not redundant. As used here, rules are considered to be the product of human communication. They manifest codes of conduct for human beings. Unlike rules, patterns are not peculiar to human beings. Thus, for our purposes, a rule is a special version of a pattern found in human systems. Rules specify codes of conduct and communication.

The Milan Associates emphasized the need to understand the rules of the game. By this, they mean that each family has unique patterns of behavior, verbal and nonverbal, that control action within that system. The task of systemic family therapists is to understand those patterns, to see that patterns control action among family members in a way that is analogous to the rules within a game. When the rules are understood, gestalts emerge. We see how relationships among needs, abilities, and roles produce unique behavior patterns that have become regularized over the life of the group. Family members do not deviate from the rules, not even when the rules are unspoken. It is probably true that for most families, deviations from the group's patterns are much less likely to occur when these rules have not been articulated. When family members are aware of their system's norms, they are in a better position to challenge and modify or replace them. When such information is not available, the system is more likely to be held hostage by its own organizational customs. Thus, an initial and fundamental strategy for systemic intervention calls for an identification of the rules. Get the rules out in the open. Make them available for inspection and tampering, for whatever is required if change is to occur.

Patterns and Rules: Systemic Suggestions

Making a pattern available to the group controlled by it is a crucial systemic intervention technique. Before this can be done, however, we must be able to *see* the pattern. First, it is important to observe the nonverbal and verbal behaviors of the group members. What we are looking for are relationships. When working with this idea, I have found it useful to concentrate on the image of a mandala, which is an historically Eastern artistic creation. A mandala is a typically circular design containing geometric shapes or smooth curves, which appear over and over again within it. Often, the shapes radiate outward from an identifiable center. The possibilities available for a mandala design are infinite, limited only by the imagination. People who doodle often produce a mandala. A theme is repeated over and over again, perhaps with several variations, throughout the time that the doodler is occupied with the task. The idea of a mandala is useful as we think of family patterns since it illustrates that the relationships are of primary importance. For example, in one of my favorite mandalas, which has been reproduced from a page in the Koran, one continuous line has been bent into rectangular shapes that lattice through one another forming a half dozen or so differently shaped pockets into which forms have been placed that appear like buds or like spinning wheels. With this mandala, as with all others, the relationship among the parts creates the pattern. The experience of relationship rather than parts can also be acquired when looking at farm country from an airplane. The relationship of the fields and crops and other arrangements creates a lovely pattern. The concentration is not on the cabbage patch as a cabbage patch, but rather on what is created by the relationship of the cabbage to the broccoli field and the carrot field.

Concentration on patterns found in mandalas and views from the air shows us the kind of thing we are looking for in living groups. We want to see how confusion moves from person to person or room to room (or corner to corner) in a tense moment. We want to see what the redundant pattern of confusion frames. When a ripple of confusion has returned to its starting point — that is, to the location where you first noticed it — can you identify a pattern that might have travelled with it, such as anger, or been framed within it, such as lack of motion by the youngest or oldest members in the group?

We search for patterns and rules here, not for causes or blame. As will be shown in a subsequent chapter, when we observe a meaningful pattern, helping it become manifest can change the system. This is what Selvini-Palazzoli and her colleagues do as they introduce counterparadoxes into a family system. Identifying and mandating a natural family pattern creates a counterpattern as a therapeutic strategy.

Before we can engage in a systemic intervention, we must learn ways of developing the ability to see patterns and group rules rather than causal sequences. Absorbed attention to designs, such as the mandala and those found in aerial views, provides an excellent start at developing skills at pattern observation. Intricate designs provide the most advanced practice at this, since one can concentrate on a small part and then see how quickly that same portion can be located elsewhere in the design. This provides effective practice in searching for redundancies. It is easiest to use this strategy in combination with practice at improving one's ability to use abductive reasoning, to think in terms of analogies. In fact, abduction is a necessary part of this activity. Using abductive reasoning while searching for visual patterns is an exercise that creates increased skill at searching for the same kind of thing within moving, behavioral patterns found in the groups of which we are a recognized part or which we are watching.

It is also helpful to realize that the relationships we are focusing on often can be represented with adjectives or adverbs as well as other forms of speech. For example, moving can be a redundant piece of an important pattern for a given family. It may be that moving about the house or yard always occurs as part of a family pattern you might come to label *trapped*. Or, it could be that a family moves from one house to another as part of a pattern, which includes other behaviors and might be labelled as *starting over*.

Sometimes, it is even useful actually to draw a pattern and begin to label the relationships (not the components) among the redundant portions within what you have drawn. Such a visual presentation can be helpful, especially when learning to think in a systemic way and when working with a particularly confusing system. When you have produced a description of relationships and have labelled the whole pattern in a meaningful way it is useful to check to see if your description contains causal inference or blame. If so, it may depend too heavily on linear thinking or on too much deductive or inductive reasoning.

DYNAMIC MODELS

Almost 2500 years ago, after careful observation, Aristotle concluded that it was the nature of all things to be at rest. He reasoned that an object would remain stationary unless someone (or something) caused it to move. Later scientific developments, originating with Newton, abandoned Aristotle's beliefs concerning motion. Nonetheless, it is true that we experience life as if it were invested in the static rather than the dynamic. As you glance around you at the moment, you can identify far more things that seem to be still than in motion. The key word here is *experience*. While we do not consciously relate to the motion around us, we have learned that motion is the norm in most instances. Newton has shown that objects will continue in motion unless their movement is interrupted. Beyond the earth's gravitational pull, for example, that chair you are sitting on would simply continue to move "forever" if it were not compelled by some energy source to turn off course, change speed, or stop. Developments in modern physics have shown that the chair can be thought of as a massed collection of atoms in a constant state of motion. Despite these newer ways of understanding our world, we continue to operate as if it is the nature of things to be at rest. We continue to experience life as if Aristotle were right.

Systems approaches tend to emphasize dynamic rather than static models. We are urged to think of the system as always in a state of flux. There are regularities, which can be thought of as patterns in all systems. In human systems, we observe rule regularities that seem to govern the action. It is important to note that there is action to govern, that movement is the "stuff" out of which systems are made. In systemic psychology, process and change are fundamental rather than matter and inertia (or stasis). Two systems-oriented colleagues of mine once noted that this perspective finds us searching for islands of stability in a sea of change. When we adopt a dynamic orientation, we believe that all relevant phenomena are moving and our "natural" tendency is to search for something static to cling to before we go under. We Westerners find it uncomfortable to operate within a world that is constantly in motion. Yet, adopting such an attitude toward the systems we work with can prove very useful as we attempt to understand and to intervene.

Dynamic vs. Static: Systemic Suggestions

Practice in observing the whole and the patterns that characterize it invariably leads to an appreciation of the dynamic qualities of the systems observed. Perhaps, that is because the movement of the pattern through the system creates the gestalt. The whole is held together by processes that create it and are characteristic of it. The exercises identified within the earlier discussions of patterns and causality will help to develop an awareness of the idea of movement and its relationship to the system. It is important to remember as you engage in these activities that change is not always progress. Often, change is just change. By labelling a certain movement as progress, we apply a value judgment. Sometimes, no such value judgment is available. When a goal is not present, it is very difficult to think of change as progress. When goals are present, the change may not represent an obvious move in the direction of the goal. These situations are particularly prevalent in systemic work, since linear thinking is kept to a minimum, as are traditional notions of causal sequence. In day-to-day systemic work, we focus most often on movement as change rather than movement as progress. Progress becomes more important across the life of a given intervention as we identify values and chart directions and goals based on them. It is only with respect to goals that a movement can be considered positive or progressive.

DISCONTINUOUS CHANGE

In the West, modern beliefs concerning the nature of change have been fashioned after the views of August Comte, the 19th century father of positivism. As I have noted elsewhere

> Comte's belief was that social change was inevitable but that it occurred gradually. His has been called an anticipatory conservatism. He is not bound to the preservation of the status quo but rather to the preservation of nature's slow incremental processes of change. This belief concerning the nature of social change is one with which today's adult generations have grown up. It expresses itself in thoughts such as "slow change will be enduring change" and "nature's method is slow, but it is progressive." In a moment of self-satisfaction toward the end of his intellectual career, Comte wrote that "all characteristics of positivism are summed up in its motto, *order and progress*, a motto which has a philosophical as well as political bearing, and of which I shall always feel glad to have been the author" (Lenzer, 1975, p. 341).
>
> Efforts to anticipate and channel an inevitable, orderly progress were the heart of Comtian philosophy and have been the cornerstone of capitalism since its beginnings. Progress was Comte's most important intellectual creation and, of course, capitalism's most revered product. (Plas, 1985, p. 312)

In a decidedly non-Comtian manner, Bateson, Prigogine, systemic psychologists, and others have been offering evidence that certain kinds of transformation are not the result of the kind of order and progress that Comte believed would always characterize lasting change. These writers talk of sudden or spontaneous change that emerges from a particular set of conditions, which seem to be present in both physical and social systems. Usually, the patterns that have been responsible for maintaining the system as a whole begin to malfunction somewhat. The old patterns have encountered new conditions that cannot be easily accommodated. Modifications of existing structures or patterns are introduced but do not work well. As a result, energy builds up and fluctuations begin to occur. The system swings in one direction, then corrects itself by swinging strongly in the opposite direction. Eventually, one of several things can happen: the system can break down, develop a set of rules (or other pattern) to guide the fluctuations, or leap to a new level of system organization. The last course is thought of as discontinuous change.

Platt (1970) talks about revolution, conversion, and falling in love as evidence of sudden transformative change within human systems. While not always explicitly adopting systemic principles, several of the newer approaches to psychotherapy are beginning to suggest that lasting, important change can occur in relatively short periods of time (cf. Strupp, 1984). The systemic family therapists rely heavily on the idea of discontinuous change. Meetings between therapists and family occur only once every month or so, and an average of only 10 sessions is not uncommon. These therapists search for a nodal point that represents the interaction of several important family rules. A counterparadox, or some other intervention, is then introduced to force the system to begin fluctuating. The therapists attempt to get the system "swinging" to establish conditions for sudden change. Thus, the therapists and their strategies become the new event (or condition) that is available to trigger change. Bateson has offered the dictum that "ongoing processes of change *feed* on the random." I commented on this phenomenon (Plas, 1985) by noting that "A new event can be part of a transformation process that finds abrupt change leading to a new level of organizational complexity. This new order emerges from, and controls, a new field" (p. 313).

Discontinuous Change: Systemic Suggestions

The idea of sudden change is one that our Western minds tend to reject out of hand. We have been culturally convinced that rapid change is "bad" change; that sudden change is unstable change. Therefore, the notion that spontaneous movement is a natural result of certain identifiable conditions is one that seems problematic to us. It actually can be a threatening idea, so controlled are we by Comte's beliefs that only slow, orderly change is "good" change. Therefore, effective work with this newer idea must begin with an inspection of the theory and research that illustrates the point. Consulting the authors mentioned here in connection with the notion of discontinuous change will prove to be time well spent. Upon acquaintance with this idea, a systemic psychologist will probably simply orient intervention strategies within a framework that recognizes sudden changes and expects them to occur. If the strategies are used thoughtfully and comprehensively, sudden change can become a reality. One does not necessarily plan for it; it simply occurs. That is, systemic psychologists do not design intervention strategies so that exactly 7 months and 7 sessions down the road the Brown family will be able to leap to a new level of system organization. What happens, however, is that the therapists organize their work with the anticipation that when systemic therapy "works," shifts can be expected relatively quickly. This expectation is remarkably different from the more traditional approaches, such as the Freudian, which expect that any really effective change will be a gradual change and take a good deal of time to mature.

STORIES

If you will practice being fictional for a while, you will understand that fictional characters are sometimes more real than people with bodies and heartbeats.
— Richard Bach

In his last book, Bateson (1979) adopted the position that mind and nature were of the same substance: that the processes and structures found in human beings were also to be found in the rest of nature, and that the organizing relations within both were of the same "stuff" as stories. That stories constitute the fabric of both mind and nature has been one of Bateson's least understood and least used ideas. Even many systemic psychologists tend to chart a course around this concept as they incorporate Bateson's thinking into their philosophies and practices. Yet, it is an idea that flows naturally into and out of the systemic epistemology. However, as I present the connections between this idea and the rest of those just listed, you should be aware that among the descriptors of systemic thought discussed in this chapter, the concept of stories is probably the only one that most systemic writers would not quickly identify as necessary. Most would not disagree that the concept is fitting, rather they might question it as a requirement. My goal here is to persuade that it is an important idea, fundamental to a complete understanding of the possibilities inherent in systemic psychology. Later in this book, I show how this concept is particularly important for adaptation of systemic methodologies within schools.

The last 20 years of Bateson's career were devoted to a search for an understanding of the patterns that connect all living things. He believed that patterns control the flow of information in a system, be the information cultural or phylogenetic. As he brought his biological-anthropological-psychological background to bear on understanding these patterns, he concluded that the characteristics of anatomy and physiology are repetitive and rhythmical across all forms of living things. Commenting on the dynamic nature of things he wrote that:

> We have been trained to think of patterns, with the exception of those of music, as fixed affairs. It is easier and lazier that way but, of course, all nonsense. In truth, the right way to begin to think about the pattern which connects is to think of it as *primarily* (whatever that means) a dance of interacting parts and only secondarily pegged down by various sorts of physical limits and by those limits which organisms characteristically impose. (Bateson, 1979, p. 13)

In an earlier chapter, I retold Bateson's favorite story about the computer that was asked if it would ever learn to think like a human. The machine's response was, "That reminds me of a story." I also offered at that point a Bateson (1979) paragraph in which he claimed that, "*thinking in terms of stories* must be shared by all mind or minds, whether ours or those of redwood forests and sea anemones" (p. 13). Both of these thoughts reflect Bateson's deep appreciation for the idea of the story as an explanatory concept. He talked about stories as "a little knot or complex of that species of connectedness which we call *relevance*" (p. 13). He thought of context or relevance as the hallmark of all forms of communication, whether it be communication among people or communication at the level of the cell or at the level of evolution. A story, for Bateson, is a complete thought. A story contains components that are relevant for one another. They are connected. He suggested that within stories, "the general fact that parts are connected in this way is at the very root of what it is to be alive" (p. 14).

It is from context, from relevance, that anything derives meaning. Bateson (1979) talked about

> An analogy between context in the superficial and partly conscious business of personal relations and context in the much deeper, more archaic processes of embryology and homology . . . whatever the word *context* means, it is an appropriate word, the *necessary* word, in the description of all these distantly related processes. (p. 15)

Bateson is trying to tell us that the pattern which connects all living things is a pattern of communication which contains parts relevant for one another in a way that allows them to have meaning as a complete thought. Since this description provides an apt definition of a story, Bateson concluded that stories constitute the pattern which connects all living things.

Like Bateson, the French philosopher Paul Riceour thinks of psychotherapy as a particularly fitting example of the regulatory power of stories. Riceour (1983) commented that the therapist's primary job is to help a client tell a coherent life story. Indeed, Riceour held that telling a coherent tale is the fundamental task for every human life. Each of our lives tells a unique tale, untold by anyone else. If we are to achieve the "good" life, we must learn to weave the parts of our lives together to tell a whole chronicle. Each of the parts of our lives must be seen as relevant to the others. Out of this relevance emerges meaning. If the parts of our lives seem unrelated then there is little meaning and, without meaning, the human personality has traditionally had difficulty conducting a rich life. Time and time again, throughout history and literature, we have been witness to stories about a human life that contained suffering and catastrophe but could be viewed to be a fruitful life by its owner as well as its observers. In all of these cases, the notion of meaning seems to have provided the beautiful fabric of being. Victor Frankl tells of the meaning some were able to weave in concentration camps. Shakespeare writes of those who squeezed meaning out of tragedy. Always, across real life and real literature, we see that it is the ability to tell a coherent, meaningful story about one's life that makes it possible — despite overwhelming odds — to live a life that its owner deems possible and valuable. Thus, for Riceour, it is, literally, the broken lives that end up at the therapist's door, where the therapist's task becomes one of aiding the client in an attempt to relate a meaningful life drama.

Lincoln and Guba (1985) quote an exemplary passage from the work of Stewart Emery.

> We put together our own personal reality. It is made up of our interpretation of our perceptions of the way things are and what has happened to us. We make some basic decisions about life when we are being born, and we add to the script and embellish it during our childhood. We end up with a view of ourselves and the world that is usually highly inaccurate, because our perceptions of the world at an early age are not accurate. . . . Out of that we put together an environment that is a perfect reflection of our view of the world.
>
> We write our script by the time we are about seven years old. Then we treat the world as if it were the back lot at Universal Studios. We pick out our sets and our props. We go to Wardrobe, which may be Sears or Macy's or Saks Fifth Avenue and choose our costumes. We select a location and begin filming the story of our life as we see it, starring US. We literally create a reality that reflects our view of the world and who we are in relation to it. (Emery, 1978, p. 73)

The obvious connection between the notion of stories and the rest of systemic thought emerges from a consideration of the idea of the life story. As we think about this human task, we are thrust toward an appreciation of systemic epistemology. The absolute, one, true reality of life can never be an important issue from a systemic point of view. Rather, it is recognized that a multiplicity of tales is possible. What *is* important are meaningful wholes, descriptions of the patterns that guide movement. Within the family therapy process, for example, a family brings a disjointed tale to the team of systemic therapists, who help to describe the patterns of communication. The therapists assist in telling the story. Since we cannot have access to ultimate, absolute reality, our challenge becomes one of seeing relationships, of knitting together incoherent parts. Our task is to identify a set of rules. Thus, we see why the Milan Associates originally talked in terms of the "rules of the game." Perhaps they could have thought just as meaningfully in terms of the "plot of the story." Human communication patterns can be seen as a story just as easily as a game. Fundamentally, these ideas are redundant.

The notion of the story is the umbrella idea for systemic psychology. Whether we think of rules or plots, the coherent tale is always what we are striving to reveal. Bateson's identification of the universal applicability of the idea of story across all living things has been problematic for some. However, his use of this umbrella concept will prove to be particularly helpful in years to come, because it is a concept that allows us to depend on epistemological beliefs that are systemic. As we talk of stories rather than "reality," we are reminded that it is not possible anywhere or anytime to speak *truth* in the positivist, Western sense of that term. The truth we speak from a systemic point of view is a contextual truth. A piece of the puzzle (or dynamic of the plot) is true if it fits, if it helps to complete the pattern from which emerges meaning.

Stories: Systemic Suggestions

Within this frame of reference, stories are the stuff of which life, as we can know it, is made. When the idea of the story is firmly in place, it constitutes the last link in the chain of systemic understanding. It is important to look for the regulatory organization within the groups we observe and attempt to change. Whether we refer to this organization as a pattern, a set of rules, a game, or a story is, ultimately, incidental. Each of these constructs, as identified here, is basically redundant with the others. There are subtle emphases contained within each term, of course, but fundamentally they refer to a single idea. For example, while a rule is a specifically human phenomenon, it is nonetheless a special case of a pattern in systemic theory. However, while these terms represent notions that are synonymous within certain contexts, the idea of the story is probably the most useful one at the present time, since it most directly forces us to employ systemic epistemology. Thus, the main suggestion here is that we learn to depend on stories as we develop descriptions and interventions that are systemic. Stories are particularly useful when working with children. Therefore, the Bateson notion of the story has peculiar relevance in the schools. Some possibilities are elaborated in the next section.

PART 2
THE MOVE INTO THE SCHOOLS

Human history becomes more and more a race between education and catastrophe.

— H. G. Wells

7
SYSTEMIC ISSUES IN THE SCHOOLS

All rising to great place is by a winding stair.
— Francis Bacon

In this country, where free education is the right of all citizens, it is not surprising that the educational enterprise becomes the field upon which we play out our deepest hopes, confusions, and incompetences. While public education has been the beginning point for most Americans, all too often we hear it said that most of us do not want to end up there, as underpaid and overhassled teachers and administrators. Yet, college-educated persons have rushed to the schools in record numbers during the past 25 years, and American television continues to portray the teacher as one of our most important heroic types. As the 20th century comes to a close, it is apparent that the public schools, in a very real way, constitute the American "frontier" even more than space. We all want to solve the "problem" of the schools. We want to be as proud of our schools as we are of the children we send there. For many, that often reduces to a somewhat uncomplicated desire for our children to get a better education than we did. For others, the issues are more intense. They see the schools as the arena in which our very values and morals are tested and redefined. Whatever position one takes, it is probably true that to a great extent what we teach to our children and how we teach it charts the future course of things more directly than any other national enterprise. It is the "how" of things that we will be most concerned with throughout the remainder of this book. The processes that prevail in schools and systemic interventions related to them will be the main focus.

America's most revered educator, John Dewey, thought that psychology's greatest challenge would ultimately reside in the schools. Dewey was an American pioneer in the fledgling science of psychology at the close of the 19th century and, unlike most others, he called for an immediate integration of the results of psychological science with the needs of education. Way back in 1899, he declared that "The main point is whether the standpoint of psychological science . . . is indifferent and opposed to the demands of education" (Hilgard, 1978, p. 66). Dewey called for carrying psychology directly into the schools, through teachers and through a group of liaison persons he referred to as *educational theorists*. As he defined it, this group seems remarkably like the school psychologists of today: professionals trained at the interface of psychological and educational theory and practice. Dewey thought that the burden of information dissemination belonged to this kind of professional. He felt that teachers would be willing and creative interpreters of psychological knowledge if given the opportunity. He wrote that

> No individual instructor can be sincere and whole hearted, to say nothing of intelligent, in carrying into effect the needed reforms, save as he genuinely understands the scientific basis and necessity of the change. (Hilgard, 1978, p. 67)

Despite Dewey's call for an organic union of education and psychology, the dream only started to become reality during the past 25 years. School psychology as we presently conceive it was not born until the 1950s when pioneers such as Susan Gray (1963) shared a vision that was not too far afield from the original Dewey hopes.

Like most new social-scientific developments, the formative years for school psychology have been turbulent (cf., "The Future of Psychology in the Schools," 1981). Still, the development of this profession has provided the needed entree to the schools for the results of psychological investigations concerned with enhancing the growth of children. At the same time, educational publishers have integrated the fruits of psychological science into creative approaches to all aspects of the curriculum. As these phenomena have progressed, administrators and curriculum specialists as well as support personnel, such as reading teachers and speech pathologists, began to sift through the psychological literature in a search for approaches to children that could be adapted for use in the schools.

Psychology has been often a disappointment for education, but it has not always defeated the educator's expectations. At this point, scientific psychology's greatest successes in the schools have been within the field of developmental psychology and testing and measurement. For example, the work of the outstanding developmentalist, Jean Piaget, revolutionized our approach to the education of young children. At the turn of the century, Dewey and others were lamenting the mainstream educational stance in this country, which found us treating our learners as "little men and little women." He believed that:

> The narrow scope of the traditional elementary curriculum, the premature and excessive use of logical analytic methods, the assumption of ready-made faculties of observation, memory, attention, etc., which can be brought into play if only the child chooses to do so, the ideal of formal discipline—all these find a large measure of their explanation in neglect of just this psychological distinction

between the child and the adult. The hold of these affairs upon the school is so fixed that it is impossible to shake it in any fundamental way, excepting by a thorough appreciation of the actual psychology of the case. (Hilgard, 1978, p. 67)

Dewey wanted us to recognize that the growth and learning patterns of children were markedly different from those of adults—and to proceed within the schools accordingly. Largely because of Piaget, we have. The impact of Piagetian psychology has been so great upon the American school curriculum that it is almost impossible to recognize it at times, so ingrained is it in the conduct of the daily business of the elementary school.

In a similar manner, the fruits of the psychological testing and measurement field have found their way to every aspect of American education, from preschool through graduate programs. As the recent testing controversy painfully reveals (cf., "The Larry P. Decision," 1980), not everyone has considered this contribution to be as valuable as that which emerged from the development specialists. However, our task here is not to engage the testing quarrel but rather to become aware of the areas in which psychology has made a difference within the schools and the areas in which it has not.

Personality and clinical psychology have been outstanding psychological subdisciplines that have not been as responsive as necessary to the needs of education. Theory and practice in clinical psychology have been oriented toward work in the mental health center or the private practitioner's office. Group work has emerged during the past 20 years but, for the most part, it has served what we have come to think of as fitness-oriented, upwardly mobile middle-class persons—a specialized clientele. Meanwhile, the schools have contained the greatest *need* for clinical services. The schools will always constitute the setting with the greatest need for applied psychological services due to the numbers involved, the breadth of difficulties to be found, and the complications of geometric proportions that occur when several disturbed children are located within the same classroom. Understandably, it is precisely within this area that expectations for scientific psychology have been highest. With good reason, parents and school personnel have had a right to expect that the science of psychology would have something to offer to the crucial issues of classroom discipline: alarming dropout rates, the unmotivated child, and school violence. It is in the area of social climate that psychology has so far failed the most. That is, the schools are largely not a great deal healthier as a place to spend 6 hours a day than they were 40 years ago. Perhaps there is a bit less paddling and physical abuse by teachers but this change has surely not resulted from the direct influence of psychological data. Rather, the courts and common sense guided this movement away from harmful corporeal punishment.

Some progress has been made through the application of behavior modification techniques. B. F. Skinner's influence has been felt in the schools.

However, behavior modification approaches have not lived up to initial expectations. Many educators and psychologists look upon these strategies as short-term solutions which emphasize extrinsic control.

Clinical psychology in the schools is still awaiting its Piaget. The personnel are there but the theory and strategies are not. School psychologists, already overburdened by extensive testing responsibilities and special education duties, would, nonetheless, greet a potent innovation in the field of school-based mental health with enthusiasm and commitment. The situation is no different now than it was when I was practicing psychology in the schools 15 years ago, the referrals on emotionally disturbed or behavior disordered children are the hardest referrals. Psychology still has the least to offer the individual child in school who experiences emotional pain and may create discomfort for those who share his or her day in the classroom. Indeed, classrooms, as natural groupings, have not been successful in gaining large amounts of scientific attention.

It is quite possible that applied psychology in the schools will benefit in a revolutionary way from input from a movement rather than input from a single genius such as Piaget. The time may well have come for a successful group-oriented psychology to be exported from other psychological settings to the public schools. Such a psychology is now available. Although it is in its infancy, systems psychology is nonetheless available for transfer to the educational setting. As Dewey said over 85 years ago, now is the moment. When we think we have hold of some psychological information that is valid and valuable, the place to carry it is into the schools.

The remainder of this chapter is devoted to a recognition of the issues that must be considered as systemic psychology is modified for use in the schools. The following chapter contains a description of school-based systemic intervention strategies and Chapter 9 then presents consideration of case composites that illustrate this method of practice. Chapter 10 describes school-based systems approaches that differ from the systemic. Chapter 11 offers comments on further possibilities.

SCHOOLS AND SYSTEMIC PSYCHOLOGY: THE ISSUES

It is valid to assume that the public schools represent the mainstream culture and that within them conventional Western thinking is typical and deeply ingrained. It would be strange if it were otherwise. We hold the schools accountable for transferring our values, attitudes, and cultural styles to our children. We expect that these public institutions will make our historically best thinking available to their charges.

As our thinking shifts, we do not expect to find it represented initially within the public schools. If systems thinking were already prevalent in the schools, they would be a substantially different place to be than they were 30 or 40 years ago. Books such as this one would be redundant with everyday experience.

That systems-oriented perspectives are beginning to find their way into the schools reveals, perhaps more than any other indicator, that this new frame of reference is coming of age. It has survived its trials in other disciplines and is ready to be tested in one of the most demanding arenas of all—the American public school.

Since mainstream Western thinking is prevalent within our educational institutions, areas of difficulty for systemic practice can be expected to permeate all aspects of daily life in these settings. Fundamentally, concern results from our Western dependence upon a linear language and linear notions of causality, as well as almost exclusive reliance on deductive and inductive reasoning and models of reality that emphasize the static essence of things and the slow nature of change. Indeed, all the points of view represented in the Chapter 6 list of systemic descriptors constitute the major areas of difficulty when attempting to transport systemic interventions to the schools. It is not a needless exaggeration to think again of the old analogy of trying to fit a square peg into a round hole. The schools are deeply entrenched in Western linear thinking. We really would not have wanted it to be otherwise during the first 80 or so years of this century. If our schools are to work, they must represent the best of what our past has chosen as real and valuable. They *must* represent mainstream thinking in a very substantial way.

Since systems-oriented thinking is making important headway in other areas of the culture, the square peg-round hole context need not be as discouraging as we might initially assume. The culture has been in the process of accommodating systems thinking for several years now. It is probably an idea whose time has come. Therefore, the schools will not be totally hostile to this new way of thinking. There will be many who have already begun to incorporate some of these ideas and many who have already been behaving in accord with some of them, either in their classrooms or in their private lives.

Despite the somewhat fertile soil on which the seeds of systemic thought are about to fall within the schools, it seems clear that the premier obstacle facing the merger of these newer ideas with the more conventional ways of thinking will probably arise out of personal discouragement. Occasionally, the attempt to design any kind of intervention strategy for a group, such as a classroom that is an identifiable part of a larger system, such as a school, can seem like an overwhelming task. In other settings, such as clinics and private practitioners' offices, there is no such clearly identifiable system available to complicate the development of therapy. Surely, there are influential groups, such as the church or extended family, but none of these typically incorporates the family within it in the same way the school does with respect to a classroom.

Thus, in addition to the discouragement that the pioneer often feels in the face of inevitable challenges, another major obstacle arises from the need to work with a group that is an integral part of a larger, geographically present, whole. A third issue revolves around definition of the ideal group that is to be the target of the intervention. To some extent, the family therapists have already experienced this problem. It is common to have difficulty in initially identifying the whole family group that needs to be included. Does the grandmother who lives on the other side of the city but communicates by telephone twice each day with the father and daughter need to be included? What about the married younger sister who has started her own family but rents an upstairs apartment from her parents? Because they have wrestled with these issues, the family therapists can offer some direction. However, the issue becomes even more salient within the schools and, in fact, is experienced in such a different way that family-oriented ways of responding to this challenge may work only clumsily within the schools. Complicating this issue is the situation identified earlier: The major difference between family and school systemic approaches lies in the inescapable fact that the most central school-based group (the classroom) is a clearly integral part of a larger system (the school), which in turn is part of another organizational structure (the school system). Thus, to work within the schools, systemic strategies must be modified to take this situation into account. Because of this, school-based systemic psychology must be systemic psychology with a somewhat different twist.

A fourth variable was alluded to earlier: Most personnel in the schools rely on Western ways of thinking about reality. In any given intervention, some of these people will be identified as members of the target group while others will not. Therefore, it is to be expected that there will be responsible parties who are ancillary to the intervention process but nonetheless influential with respect to the members of the targeted group. Upon first inspection, this factor may seem to have already been accounted for, as we noted that the focus-group will most often be a recognizable part of a larger administrative and/or organic unit. However, while this fourth issue is complementary to the second, it is not redundant with it. This can be seen in relation to the family therapy model: All responsible parties who are not initially identified as part of the target group (the family) are therapists. Typically, no other responsible persons are to be considered in an immediate sense within the family model of systemic practice. The family generally comes to a clinic or private office and the intervention proceeds. In the schools, certain persons must be identified as responsible and/or interested parties, and yet they will initially not be considered a part of the target group or the intervention team. A fundamental reason why this fourth issue is not synonymous with the second is that the second refers to a clearly identifiable larger unity, which can conceivably contain (a) the targeted group, (b) responsible and/or interested parties who are not part of the focus-group or the intervention team, and (c) other individuals who are members of the larger system but are not expected to have salient influence during the life of the intervention. In the fourth issue, we must focus on individuals (although, later on, they may be conceptually seen as part of one of the groups of interest). As we consider the second issue, we think in terms of organic and/or administrative wholes such as classroom, school, or system.

A fifth issue concerns the make-up of the intervention team. Obviously, in most cases, the team will not be constituted from a group of psychologists who operate outside the system. In fact, it is most likely that some of the team members will not be psychologists at all; rather, they may be other support personnel within the school system.

A sixth challenge relates to the ethical needs of the situation. Systemic intervention calls for a thoughtful and detailed stance toward ethics. While the school system is no different from the clinic or private office in terms of the need for ethical behavior, work within a larger system always presents unique ethical dilemmas, since it is not always clear who the client is. The need to consider this question is not solely germane to systems-oriented interventions. All psychological interventions carried out within the schools (or any other institution such as a prison) require special attention to clear identification of the client. Within the family therapy model, the issue is rarely raised. The client is the family. However, if the classroom is the focus-group, is the classroom the client, or the principal who made the referral, or the parents of the children, or who? This decision is never an automatic one. Adequate ethical conduct depends upon an appropriate identification of the client within school-based systemic intervention.

APPROACHES TOWARD ISSUES UNIQUE TO THE SCHOOLS

Systemic work within public education institutions must be conducted somewhat differently than in clinics due to the specific issues just cited: the focus-group's identity as part of a larger system; identification of the group; influential members of the system who are ancillary to the intervention; the make-up of the intervention team; and, special ethical considerations. Subsequent to a pragmatic treatment of these issues, it will be possible to identify appropriate modifications of existing systemic techniques that will reflect the influence of those descriptors of systemic thought considered at length in Chapter 6.

Focus-Group's Position Within a Larger System

Most of the time, the group identified as the focus-group will be an entity, such as an intact classroom or history class or, perhaps, a reading group. Thus, usually, the focus-group will be geographically as well as culturally contained within a larger system, such as a school. If an entire school is chosen as the target, it too will be contained within a larger system: the complete school system. While not geographically surrounding the school in the same way that the school surrounds the classroom, the total school system is, nonetheless, the cultural host for the individual school. Since this situation is so different from that faced by the systemic family therapist, the conventional methods of family practice will not work unless they are tailored to fit the uniqueness of this situation.

First, the intervention team must establish to which larger system the focus-group belongs. It is obvious that a classroom group is nested within a school and, thus, there will be an automatic tendency to quickly identify the school as the system most importantly connected with the focus-group. Occasionally, this assumption will be incorrect. Therefore, an important criterion should be addressed before arriving at an identification of the host system. If consulted each time, this criterion will prevent the costly errors that inevitably ensue from a false identification of the larger group. The most important system of which the focus-group is a part is always the next larger group with which the focus-group shares resources. Material and nonmaterial supplies flow back and forth between the focus-group and the larger system. Watch for important exchanges of supplies, such as books, pencils, and so forth, as well as instrumental support, such as substitute teachers, help with grading papers, and the like. There is an organic connection between the focus-group and the larger system. At all times, it is wise to keep in mind that the larger system could be conceived of as the focus-group if that were to meet intervention needs and goals. Thus, it is helpful if the intervention team members constantly remind themselves of the organically important position of the focus-group within the larger system.

It is always necessary to question the focus-group as to which larger system it is most immediately connected with and to ask this question in at least two ways: What is the next larger school-based group of which this group is a part? From which other group in this school system are you most likely to receive supplies and support when you need it? Asking the group members in this way helps to avoid those relatively rare, but nonetheless important, identification errors that can occur when only the intervention team members are involved in locating this crucial relationship.

The presence of such an organically important host system forces us to modify conventional systemic strategies. The major reason for this is that from time to time — usually when team members will least appreciate the situation — focus-group members will cease functioning as members of that group and begin to participate as an organic member of the larger system. If this occurs during an intervention strategy, it can precipitate the failure of the method if not anticipated and considered thoroughly relative to the strategy in operation. In the following chapter, the reader will find that the systemic strategies created for use in the schools are heavily dependent on a recognition of the need to consider the larger system of which the focus-group is an integral part.

Identification of the Group

Clear identification of the focus-group is absolutely necessary for successful intervention. In the case of family therapy, the identification of the family group is somewhat tricky. In the case of the schools, identification of the focus-group is more than just tricky; it is challenging. The first rule to remember is that the make-up of the focus-group within the schools is always available for change. New students move into the system; other students move out. Substitute teachers may be around for a day or a month. Support personnel, such as reading teachers, come and go. While the members of families occasionally change, as stepparents enter a family or children leave town, these changes are relatively infrequent compared to what we can expect within a typical school system during any given 9-month school year. It will be the rare instance when membership of a focus-group remains stable over the course of an academic year.

It is also important to remember that the nature of public education is such that the membership of most intact groups changes each school year. Therefore, if a classroom unit is to be the focus-group it is important to begin the intervention in September, at the beginning of the 9-month period when the focus group will remain intact. Some organic units within a system will carry over from year to year and, thus, it is not as important that the intervention begin in autumn. For example, in many schools, the teaching staff remains fairly stable from one year to the next. If the teacher group is the focus-group of systemic intervention, a 3-month summer vacation can be used profitably within the design of the intervention and it is possible to begin at any point during the school year.

Identification of the focus-group must be dependent upon an appreciation of what we mean in systemic psychology by an organic unity. In an organic human group, affective as well as instrumental and material resources are available for exchange or for withholding. The members of the group identify with the group — for better or worse. They may not *like* being a member of this group but they are well aware that they *are* a member of this group. The members of the group are in a dependent relationship with one another; that is, they need to relate to one another as a result of geographical or cultural expectations and personal needs. Esteem and caring are important resources that group members would appreciate receiving from other members of the group. (Remember, for purposes of identification it is not necessary for members actually to receive these resources; rather, it is important to realize there is a perceived or felt need to receive them from members of this group.)

It is unwise to try to forge a focus-group from among persons who are not genuinely members of an organic unity. Systemic intervention depends upon the presence of a natural system. While it may seem logical that a given group within the school might be an appropriate focus-group, it is essential that the group members behave toward the group in the ways just outlined. The members must accept the identification as members of the natural unity you are attempting to circumscribe. In almost all school systems, classrooms and coaching staffs will fit the criteria. In almost every system, all 10-year olds and all tenured teachers will not fit the criteria. Somewhere between these two examples of intact and nonintact groups, lies most of the natural systems that lend themselves to systemic work. The task of identifying the group is not an automatic one. However, it is not an impossibly difficult one, if the criteria just mentioned are used in a systematic fashion.

Once the team has developed a general idea about the nature of the focus-group, it is important to establish who is a member of the group and who is not. This should be done by name and by functional role in the school. It is important to refrain from saying that all of Mr. Hunter's third period social studies students are members. As you begin (with Mr. Hunter) to name each student, it will become apparent whether each is actually a part of the group. For example, in some cases you might find that a boy is on the class role but has been cutting the class every period for the first three weeks of school, or a student may be expelled or ill so much of the time that other members do not consider her to be an integral member of the group. It is important that group membership be an accepted fact for each person involved. Borderline members need to be addressed on a case-to-case basis. When a borderline member has been identified as a member of the out-group, intervention sessions should never occur when that person is temporarily present within the group.

A final stage of identification should involve a direct confrontation of the membership issue at the beginning of the first intervention session. At that time, each person should have the opportunity to voice his or her feelings regarding membership. The team members must be sensitive to the member who ridicules and rejects the group but is, nonetheless, an integral member of the whole. An analogous situation is sometimes found within family work where a child will complain about the family, indicating that he or she has never really been a part of it and has no use for it. Obviously, in such a case, the energy comes out of the child's important identity as part of the group and not out of a sense of borderline identity.

It is not unusual for this identification process to take several hours of focused work on the part of two to four team members prior to the first intervention session. If it can be concentrated within the first weeks of school, so much the better for those interventions that must be contained within the conventional 9-month school year. In some cases, this will not be possible since it will take several weeks for bonds to be formed among group members. If the group requires time for natural formation, it must be afforded that time. Premature group identification creates needless difficulties and, in the long run, will require additional effort and time because these initial identification processes probably will need to be repeated.

At regularly scheduled intervals throughout the life of the intervention, group membership should be reestablished. This requires team member and focus-group member participation and accord. It is to be expected that membership will fluctuate somewhat. The addition or deletion of a member can provide an opportunity for probing the system in a neglected dimension or for designing a strategy to capitalize on the chance occurrence of a change in membership. Some of these opportunities should become easier to visualize during discussions of specific strategies, which occur in the next chapter.

Influential Persons Who Are Not Members of the Focus-Group

Earlier, we considered the unique situation in which the focus-group is a member of a larger organic whole. In addition to considering the larger system as system, it is helpful to relate to some of its members as individuals throughout the life of the project. For example, a school principal may not be a member of the group with which you are working. At times, the principal will function as a member of the larger system, be it the school or the next higher level organizational unit. The principal functions in this way in exchanges involving the system culture or resources. At other times, however, the principal will seem to be functioning more as an individual. I have found it helpful to make this distinction, and I found it a relatively easy one to make. When the principal seems to be functioning primarily out of his or her own expectations, needs, and personal characteristics, it is sometimes more helpful to think of this person as an individual relating to the focus-group rather than as the larger system relating to the focus-group. For example, some principals have a tight administrative style. As individuals, they feel more comfortable knowing everything, even the smallest detail, that relates to life within their schools. As an interested principal adopts this style with respect to the systemic intervention team, it will be helpful to think of the principal as an influential individual at those moments rather than as a representative of the system culture. This particular phenomenon is one often experienced by those who do family work. It is not uncommon, for example, that a neighbour will get involved with a family in an important way, representing no other group, only herself or himself as an individual.

The role of parents vis-a-vis the intervention strategy is best conceived within the issue at hand. Parents are influential individuals; yet, they do not function as part of a larger system to which the focus-group is organically connected. At all times, the rights and needs of parents are important for all activities that occur within the schools. Systemic intervention is no exception. Parents can affect the course of the intervention in positive, negative, or neutral ways. It is crucial that their good will and support be involved as much as possible. An agreement concerning the best way to approach parents (when that is necessary) should be worked out with the school principal, who is administratively responsible for the focus group.

In general, no particular strategies flow from a consideration of this issue that need attention at this point. What is most important is that the team make itself aware of when an influential person is acting as an individual and when that person is functioning as a representative of the larger system. Such a distinction can be very useful during confusing or tense moments, which may arise during the course of the intervention. Since the focus-group is available to a larger unit, to individuals within that unit, and to parents, it must be expected that meaningful involvement with these unities and persons will occur from time to time. Powerful involvements with some of these individuals will produce more effective interventions.

Make-up of the Intervention Team

In the family systems model, the team is conventionally made up of four mental health professionals, who share a private practice or work together within a mental health agency. In the schools, the situation can be remarkably different, since many school systems are not served by pupil personnel teams. In a large percentage of the cases, school psychologists, counselors, and social workers function independently with little or no contact. Occasionally, psychologists from nearby mental health agencies act as consultants to a school system. In other situations, guidance counselors are available within the schools, but only for high school use. In cases where support personnel teams are already available and functioning, school nurses and attendance officers may play an important team role. Thus, it is clear that each school situation is a unique one. In some settings, an interested interventionist may find an embarrassment of riches among the available support personnel who might be interested in crafting a systemic intervention team. In others, it may seem at first glance as if no help is available at all.

The important thing to remember when anticipating the construction of a systemic team is to keep one's options open. Be careful not to foreclose on certain possibilities too quickly. It is conceivable that gifted interventionists may be available but obscured from notice because of the nature of the roles they occupy. It is not obvious, for example, that a teacher or principal might make a fine systemic interventionist. We tend to think of these roles as too time-consuming to permit taking on yet another responsibility. However, some persons who have real potential for this kind of work can be found in these roles. Fortunately, they need not be overlooked as possible team participants since the actual conduct of systemic intervention will usually take place within the schools during only 8–10 sessions, which are spread across a 9-month period. Admittedly, the preparation time for systemic practice in general, as well as any given case, can require considerable time. However, there are accruing returns. In the beginning, large amounts of reading and planning time may be needed but, as interventions are attempted and carried through to conclusion the team participants gain a wealth of experience and subsequent cases may require less reading and thinking time. It is wise to caution ourselves, nonetheless, that, since systemic thinking runs counter to mainstream thought, truly successful systemic intervention will probably require a larger than usual commitment to processes of dialogue among team members. No matter how "good" we get at systemic thinking, reminders concerning the need to "clean up our language" seem always to be necessary. Until recursive, acausal ways of thinking gain a greater hold on the Western imagination, this will continue to be true. Therefore, while the time needed for meeting with the focus-group may be severely restricted relative to other forms of intervention, the needs of team members for continual dialogue usually will require larger amounts of time than anticipated.

The characteristics of persons who make good systemic interventionists seem to include

- patience
- caring
- interest in adopting systemic perspectives
- ability to adopt systemic perspectives
- ability to keep one's ego distant from the process
- self-control
- enjoyment of the mystery
- enjoyment of the game
- commitment

- sense of humor
- ethical standards
- ability to work within a team format

Formation of a systemic team should begin with a discussion group. At least 20 sessions should be scheduled across a period of 4–6 months. Depending upon the level of sophistication available with respect to systemic concepts, these sessions usually will require 2–3 hours apiece. It takes time for these newer ideas to germinate and begin to make sense. Since success depends upon learning a new way of thinking, commitment to an understanding of the idea is absolutely necessary. If this initial stage of the process were to be deemphasized or cut short, there is danger that the interventions will go awry and even be unsalvageable. People who work with systemic ideas tend to make their biggest errors as they apply techniques before they have acquired an adequate understanding of the concepts on which the strategies are based. Conducting this initial study group with four to eight persons is best. Not all participants will be in a position to become part of the team. Those who do not can provide important feedback later on and can contribute to a general sense of understanding of systemic notions within the larger school system. I recommend that at least two entire sessions be devoted to the following topics:

- history and varieties of systemic intervention
- epistemology
- language
- recursion and linearity
- acausality and causality
- other descriptors of systemic thought (see Chapter 6)
- strategies and techniques
- ethics
- issues unique to the team's school setting

The works cited throughout this book will provide an adequate reading list—at least an initial one. When consulting the family literature, the team should routinely translate intriguing ideas and strategies into manageable adaptations for the schools. A consideration of the unique school-related issues raised above will always help to make such adaptations viable. Each strategy should be evaluated in terms of its suitability for transition to intervention work with a system within a system, which is influenced by that larger system as well as potent individuals from within or without it.

The Outside Consultant. I recommend that the team work with a consultant from outside the school system for the first 2 years of implementation of this model. The consultant should be a family or school-oriented therapist who knows the systemic literature and has had some experience within this approach. Working with such a person will impressively maximize the likelihood of success—in understanding the model as well as implementation. A surprisingly small investment can reap great rewards; an hour or two of consultation time per month will be quite adequate and can be obtained in most states from a licensed person for well under $100 per hour. Persons (usually psychologists or social workers) with some expertise in systemic work are now available in most major cities. Communities that do not have such persons working within them usually can bring someone in from another location for one or two hours per month.

The advantages of working with an outside consultant for awhile are substantial: it is easier to become aware of where your mistakes and hitches lie; the larger school system and the individuals within it feel more comfortable in attempting new procedures when a consultant is available to monitor the process; the arrangement provides for a place to turn when frustration and confusion arise; learning comes easier and with a greater sense of security. I would not recommend beginning systemic work without arranging for this kind of assistance.

Ethics: Who the Clients Are and How Best to Care About Them

As soon as a focus-group has been identified and its membership delineated, the team should concentrate on defining who the client is. Within most mental health codes of professional ethics it is important to ascertain this, since major responsibilities are owed to the client. For example, the client's confidentiality may not be breached; client welfare is to be safeguarded at all times.

The issue of the nature of the client has always been a tricky one for those who practice psychology in the schools. Certain laws expect that the schools act *in loco parentis* and other laws grant parents sole rights over matters affecting their child. Thus, some believe that the parent is always the client for those who conduct interventions in the schools. Certain contrasting ethical guidelines call for the school-based professional to consider the needs of the employer as primary. From this point of view, the school is always the client. Child advocates stress that children are the most vulnerable members of our society and that ethical obligations dictate a view that the child is *always* the client—no matter what.

The American Psychological Association appointed a task force some years ago to investigate similar issues with respect to intervention and research work within the prisons (Moynihan, 1972). Their report provides a helpful way of looking at the issues and I recommend that all persons engaged in systemic work in the schools consult the report prior to beginning with a focus-group.

The issues are not clear cut. When deciding who the client is in school-based systemic work, it is important that the team forge a group position. In my view, it is practical to think in terms of primary and secondary responsibilities. I further believe that the focus-group always must be considered the client because good intervention cannot proceed without an assurance of the confidentiality and commitment afforded the primary client. However, other groups and individuals deserve, and must receive, secondary attention. These include parents and such persons as the school principal, when the focus group is contained within a single school.

The confidentiality and the welfare of the client become the two most important issues for consideration in terms of the identified client. The client's confidence must not be breached. This means that the thoughts and feelings shared with the team members must remain solely with the team members. The other interested systems and parties will need to be informed that this ethical guideline will function in an important way throughout the intervention, and thereafter as well. Early in the process, team members should decide to what extent confidentiality is to be afforded to secondary groups and individuals. Once these decisions have been made, all parties should be informed of the decisions that will guide the team's ethical conduct. Secondary groups or individuals should not be placed in the position of expecting confidential treatment that the team is unwilling or unable to deliver.

The ethical stance associated with the welfare of the client requires that all aspects of the intervention be designed with the primary and immediate purpose of benefiting the client. When the needs of the focus-group and those of other groups or individuals conflict, it is the needs of the focus-group that should be served.

The issue of informed consent from parents should be handled in the routine way that such matters are dealt with in the host system when group interventions are involved. In many cases, school systems do not gain parental consent when classroom groups are the target of intervention. The reasoning here is that individual attitudes and behaviors are not the target of change; therefore, parental permission is not required. It is particularly true in systemic intervention that individuals are not the target of intervention. Thus, it is conceivable that this approach to informed consent might meet the team's goals. However, no matter what policy is in operation within the school system, it is important that the team consider the issue, decide what approach makes the most sense given the intervention goals and the welfare of the focus-group, and subsequently work to adapt the local policy if that seems necessary.

There is a less formal, but nonetheless important, ethical issue that demands as much attention in systemic intervention as do confidentiality and welfare of the client. This is the issue of respect for the focus-group and its members. Blaming individuals or the group for attitudes or behaviors simply is not a part of a systemic perspective. Rather, a fitting attitude would complement that adopted by the Milan Associates as they engage in work with families: enjoyment of the process and enjoyment of the "players" who share the game. The systemic approach cannot work without a great deal of respect present for the clients. Strategies must be implemented with genuine caring and respect for the members of the focus-group. I have observed that when this is not the case, systemic therapy with families devolves into a meaningless series of techniques. The therapists involved almost always end up at genuine odds with the family—or worse, involved in a battle of wills. When team members begin to say things like "He's the one who is really rocking the boat all the time," not only is linear and causal thinking a problem but also a tendency toward blame, and blame will eventually render the intervention impotent if not checked in time. Team members should be vigilant in watching for signs of disrespect or blame directed toward members of the group. Systemic practice cannot continue in the presence of this mindset because it is the result of conventional linear ways of construing reality. I have found it pragmatic to encourage an attitude of love and caring toward the clients. Such an attitude makes it a bit more difficult for the conventional Western ways of construing reality to be in control of the situation. It is more difficult for linear causal models to get a toehold when an acceptance of what "is" forms the leading edge of the team's mindset.

8

SCHOOL-BASED SYSTEMIC METHODOLOGY

If you think education is expensive, try ignorance.
— Anonymous

Harvard's Sarah Lawrence Lightfoot is one of this country's most heartening educational pioneers. The schools she worked with think she has made a difference. While apparently not directly schooled in systems psychology, she nonetheless reflects these perspectives in her writing and in her work. Lightfoot talks about portraiture as a qualitative approach to research in the schools. As a way of provoking change, she develops verbal portraits of a school, which tend to have an important impact on the system and its individual members. As she describes her portraiture processes, she sounds like Bateson-turned-educator:

> Sometimes the repetitive refrains, the persistent themes, were not voiced as forcefully and clearly as they were at Carver and St. Paul's, but I found that they emerged at all of the schools I visited and became the central dimensions of the portraits. It is in finding the connections between these themes that the observer begins to give shape to the portrait. . . . The creative and analytic task of portraiture lies in exploring and describing these competing and dissonant perspectives, searching for their connections to other phenomena, and selecting the primary pieces of the story line for display.
> One searches for coherence, for bringing order to phenomena that people may experience as chaotic or unrelated . . . . Decisions are made about what must be left out in order to pursue what one thinks are central and critical properties. The piecing together of the portrait has elements of puzzle building and quilt making. How does one fit the jagged, uneven pieces together: When the pieces are in place, what designs appear? A tapestry emerges, a textured piece with shapes and colors that create moments of interest and emphasis. (Lightfoot, 1983, pp. 15–16)

The practice of systemic psychology in the schools is conceptually well within the Lightfoot tradition. While she has not explicitly addressed the important issue of the observer's epistemology, she has clearly recognized the observer's role in the construction of the reality of the school. She claims an intellectual debt to the philosopher Michael Polanyi, who talks about "the 'personal participation' of the knower in all acts of understanding" (Lightfoot, 1983, p. 380). Beginning with an appreciation of this fundamental systemic (or transactional) point of view, she naturally arrives at conclusions reminiscent of much that we have been discussing here. There is an emphasis on recursive processes, a view toward the dynamic rather than static, an appreciation of rhythms and patterns (and patterns which connect), and an investment in the story as a medium for scientific-professional expression. While concentrating on one of her pieces, the reader begins to appreciate the movement in a school as well as the rich meshing of cultural themes and the mechanisms that express them. An awareness of the observer's contributions to what is observed is always present. A reading of Lightfoot (1978; 1983) is, thus, essential for those who are interested in forging a union between systemic psychology and public education. In fact, her work is the perfect place to start: it provides an effective prime for the pump.

SYSTEMIC STRATEGIES FOR THE SCHOOLS

The strategies to be described have been designed to promote a context within which a clearly identified natural group can learn to talk out loud about the heretofore unspoken rules of communication that govern the action in the group.

The Referral

It is important that the initial referral receive detailed attention. Typically, the referrals for psychological or social services within a school system come from persons who do not consider themselves to be in need of service. Principals may refer children or teachers to the school psychologist in order that certain problems within the child or within the classroom "get fixed." Teachers refer children for learning or emotional problems. When family problems are suspected, a school nurse or principal might contact a social worker. Within the traditional model of psychological practice within the schools, the referral source is not part of the focus of intervention. However, within systemic psychology, this referring person will often be a part of the focus-group that is to receive services. Therefore, it is important that the referral be given special attention. The team will be interested in the extent to which the referring person considers himself or herself part of the "problem" or potentially part of the solution. It will be important to identify the formal and informal relationships of this person to the individual or group referred for service. The referring person's level of affect associated with the problem and understanding of the dynamics involved are crucial, as is a clear picture of the extent to which the referring person actually believes that something can be done to alleviate the situation. All of these issues should be considered within a systemic frame of reference, where the search is for patterns and rules rather than causal sequences of behavior.

Establishing the Focus-Group

During the first stages of the intervention process, there is a need to consult with the referring person, the referred person, and any other individuals identified by these two as important to the processes of interest. This stage receives more attention within systemic school work than it does with family intervention. These individuals will direct the team toward appropriate identification of the focus-group. We need to know within which group the troublesome behavior typically occurs. It is important to pay strict attention to the responses to this question. One of the informants may report that the behavior emerges only during remedial sessions, which occur outside the classroom; yet, this informant might desire that intervention proceed within the regular classroom or, perhaps, with the child alone. An important choice is to be made here. The remedial education group could be the natural focus-group with which to be concerned. However, it is also possible that the referring person, a teacher perhaps, may be interested in the behavior of this particular child only as an expression of concern about what goes on within the classroom, the system most important to him or her. The relevant questions to be asked during moments of confusion within these initial stages are "To what groups do both the referring person and referred person belong? If this group were to be focus-group, is it probable that the identified discomforts could be changed?" Thus, it is crucial that the referring person be kept involved long enough for satisfactory identification of the appropriate group and long enough for the team to gain assurance that intervening with this particular group will open the targeted behaviors to the intervention effort. The team's intention, of course, will not be to focus on these targeted behaviors. Rather, it is important to know that they are available to the focus-group, so that they can become clues for the identification of a potent nodal point later in the process.

The team should assume that any collection of people within the school can become the focus-group. If applied carefully, the criteria described in a preceding section will reveal the relevant group. It needs to be a natural unity and it is important that affective resources be prized within the group and that the members identify with it. Once a tentative identification has been made, the focus-group will be asked to explore its identity as a group during the initial stages of the first session.

If at any point in this process confusion should reign supreme, the procedure should be undertaken all over again—beginning with the referral source. A wealth of information will be gained by repeating these stages and, thus, there is no need to worry that time is being wasted. Intervention is proceeding even though the focus-group has not yet been convened in the presence of the team. It is important to remember that systemic intervention can work more quickly than other types of intervention and that fewer sessions with the clients are required. Actual meeting time is often not as important as the preliminary identification of patterns and the planning-for-intervention, which is the hallmark of systemic strategy.

The Team

Ideally, the team should contain four members. Two of the team members will have direct contact with the focus-group during the intervention sessions; the other two will not. It will not be possible in the schools to place the second two team members behind a one-way mirror, as is often the case in family therapy. Such equipment is not available in schools and, thus, strategies must be used that do not rely on this physical arrangement.

Without the one-way mirror, the team loses a double-image of the group's dynamics. That is, it is not possible for those who are outside the intervention room to comment from personal experience on the process. Because this important vantage point is lost, the out-of-room team must be especially vigilant in helping the direct-contact team gain additional perspectives — to stand back to look at the situation from a variety of other angles. It is advisable to station the out-of-room team members close to the action, so that consultations can be arranged as planned or as necessary.

Within the school model, the out-of-room group can function quite easily in the manner of Papp's Greek chorus (see Chapter 5). There will be times when prearranged knocks on the door can call one or both direct-contact team members away. Other meetings within the intervention hour can be arranged by the direct-contact team. It is important that the function of the two groups of intervention persons be clearly identified. The contact team should function as the on-site persons, who become involved with the focus-group, and, in the Papp sense, mediate between it and the Greek chorus outside the room. The out-of-room team presents the focus-group with other realities, which need to be dealt with and acknowledged. This group can seem to have access to an objective "truth" about things. Papp's Greek chorus variation of systemic team work is particularly suited to the schools since the out-of-room team mirrors the presence of a larger system that absorbs the focus-group and contains culture and attitudes to which the focus group must be responsive. No matter what natural group is being worked with in the schools, there will always be a larger system, geographically present, to which the focus-group is valuable and accountable. The out-of-room team is superbly suited to represent the realities of system-within-system living. Thus, of the group of four interventionists, the members of the out-of-room team should be the furthest removed, emotionally and physically, from the members of the focus-group. It would not do, for example, to have a teacher be a member of an out-of-room team for a focus group contained within his or her classroom group. The members of the focus-group could have access to the teacher when intervention sessions were not taking place and, thus, could experience direct influence from and toward the teacher. This situation would weaken the potential effectiveness of the intervention team. The ideal situation would be for members of the out-of-room team to be staff members from another section of the school or from another school altogether. Members of the direct-contact team should not be persons who have direct contact with the focus-group on a daily basis. Fewer conflicts of interest or role confusions will occur if members of the team have no direct involvement with the focus-group at all. Thus, support personnel, such as psychologists and social workers, are potentially the best systemic team members. However, persons in other roles can occasionally prove to be excellent additions to a team, particularly if they engage in systemic intervention in one school while staffing a school role (such as principal or teacher) in another school within that system. More explicit discussion of the functioning of the double teams will be presented.

Working Method

Most interventions will require 8–10 sessions, spaced at 1-month intervals. It is important that time be available so that the intervention can work its way through the system. Team members should not yield to the demand or desire to schedule extra sessions when things seem to be going awry or don't seem to be changing at all. One of the most difficult things for systemic interventionists to learn is to remain calm and move slowly when apparent emergencies arise. This is particularly true in the schools, where staff members will add additional pressure for the team to be responsive to momentary difficulties. Thus, it is important that an agreement be reached, in the beginning, that such problems will be handled within the normal course of school policy, not within the systemic intervention process. All those who feel responsible for the focus-group should be a party to this agreement. Such preliminary planning will serve the process well as the intervention proceeds. In addition to making these advance arrangements with responsible individuals and systems surrounding the focus-group, it is important that team members realize that, occasionally, interventionists can provide for their own defeats. Moving slowly and sticking to the intervention schedule maximizes the chances of success within the systemic model. An old expression has it that "nothing is ever served as hot as it is cooked."

This reasoning applies to momentary crises within all groups, and the schools are certainly no exception.

The conventional systemic schedule can be adapted to the schools with little trouble. Prior to the session, the double teams should meet as a group in order to design preliminary descriptive hypotheses and plan strategies for the session. Contact points between the two teams during the session should be decided upon at this time. This meeting will last from 1-2 hours and will be followed by the intervention session, which should last no more than 1 or $1\frac{1}{2}$ hours. At the prearranged end of that part of the session, the contact team will meet with the out-of-room team in order to work toward an understanding of the rules of the game and potential nodal points, as well as identification of the systemic strategy that will be carried back to the focus-group. This session must occur immediately after the direct contact session and the contact team should return to the focus-group within the hour to relay the team's decisions. In some cases within the schools, scheduling of classes and so forth will not permit this prompt return to the focus-group. When this is the case, the contact team should return to the focus-group the very next time it meets. If such a meeting is not to occur for more than 48 hours, a special meeting with the focus-group will need to be arranged. Subsequent to this event, the intervention team should meet in order to process the entire intervention episode. When the parts of the episode are spread across more than 2 days, some of the potency of the intervention can evaporate.

Strategies

The strategies most useful for the schools tend to be those that provoke discontinuous change and, yet, do not occasion disturbed concern in other parts of the larger system. Within the schools, a conservative approach is often best. When dealing with a system within a system (within a system), it is always crucial to confine, as much as possible, aspects of the intervention to those directly involved. The rules of the game that operate within the focus-group represent only one set of rules that govern the actions within the school. There are a myriad of other rules and a myriad of other games. Thus, it is crucial to consider the ripples through the wider system that will occur as the intervention gains momentum. Only ripples that can be accommodated by the larger system should be instigated. Usually, this means that modest and simple strategies, rather than flashy and complicated ones, will get the best results in the schools. Fortunately, the theory and method are potent enough that modest and simple strategies can be more than sufficiently effective for the goals associated with school-based interventions.

With these comments in mind, I recommend that five strategies constitute the core of systemic intervention in the schools: recursive questioning, storytelling, positive connotation, prescription, and ritual. The first two are oriented primarily toward diagnosis, while the latter two are directed toward intervention. Positive connotation provides a focus on both diagnosis and intervention. In the hands of committed interventionists, a thoughtful and efficient use of these strategies, which results from grounding in a sophisticated understanding of systemic theory, can produce meaningful results in most schools. All strategies are designed to provoke metacommunication: to make it possible for the group to begin talking about its unspoken rules of communication.

Recursive questioning is a common systemic strategy for work with families. Various authors interpret the concept in somewhat different ways; the major writers cited in previous chapters should be consulted as the team forms its approach to this strategy (cf. Penn, 1982; Selvini-Palazzoli, Boscolo, Cecchin, & Prata, 1980). These writers speak of circular questioning which is best described as recursive questioning in the sense in which the term *recursive* was defined in Chapter 6. Thus, recursive questioning refers to questioning that is not linear; these questions feed back upon the issue at hand. They call for abductive rather than linear (deductive and inductive) thought processes. Recursive questions are not causal questions. In Bateson's terms, recursive questioning elicits differences that make a difference. For example, an interventionist might ask the focus-group members which other classroom group they would like to be a member of—and why. The why part of the question is particularly crucial. When causal connotations are eliminated, the second part of the response gives information about the difference that makes a difference. For example, a child might note that two friends are unalike because one likes to tell lies and the other does not. This kind of information is fundamental for an understanding of the rules that govern the game.

Penn thinks of circular questioning as a way of gaining information about the different ways members experience the family before and after the introduction of the family's "problem." This is a particular form of a "difference which makes a difference" question. It calls for specific information concerning changes in ways of relating after the group has experienced a difficulty. A question such as "What is the difference in the way this group works now that the girls in the class keep important secrets to themselves?" or "What's been different since Mrs. Ross and Danny had that argument in class?"

Another category of recursive question has been called *gossiping in the presence*. This form can be used effectively by asking individuals to comment on the relationship of two or more other individuals within the group. As the intervention team is beginning to learn to field these questions, it is wise to use gossiping in the presence with a focus only on subgroups. Consider a question such as "What are the ways in which the teacher and the boys in this class communicate to one another?" Another version might be "What are the kids like who enjoy reading a lot? Describe them." Like other forms of recursive questioning, this kind of inquiry reveals patterns and redundancies that will help the team to locate a good nodal point for intervention impact. As the team becomes more experienced, it can effectively work with gossiping in the presence directed toward individuals. For example, a team member might ask if Laura's relationship with Misty might be an important thing for Mickey (or someone else) to comment on. A general form of the question might be something to the effect of "Sashi, when you look at Bill and Nancy's relationship, what do you see?" I recommend that the individualized form of gossiping in the presence be reserved for later in the intervention plan or when the team has gained good experience with circular questioning in general. The more individualized form may raise the level of threat somewhat, in that one member of the focus-group is asked to reveal personal opinions about the relationship that two others experience. This kind of question can quickly lead to a higher level of intimacy than when subgroups are named rather than individuals.

As responses to the recursive questions become available, the team's task is to catch the redundancies, to scan the responses in a search for the rules of communication in this group. Circular questioning brings to the fore those dynamics responsible for holding the group together as a group. They do not typically elicit causal statements; rather, they reveal similarities and differences and the "glue" that binds together people and communication mechanisms within this group. Such questions should be liberally strewn throughout the intervention session. It is not necessary to direct them toward the issue or person that prompted the referral. In fact, it is often best to ignore the referring issue. It is much more important to gain an understanding of a more fundamental set of rules for this group. Usually, the presenting problem is an expression of something more important and more pervasive. Concentrating the questioning on the referral situation tends to create a straw person, which will provide distraction rather than illumination.

Storytelling is the strategy least often used within systemic family work and one of the most useful of strategies for school-based intervention. The storytelling strategy is based on Bateson's belief that the stuff of stories is the stuff of the reality with which we deal on a daily basis. Stories can be one of the most influential of patterns that connect other patterns. Storytelling provides almost instantaneous information concerning the rules of the game and the themes that bind the group together.

I recommend such questions as "Kelly, if this group were acting out a fairy tale, which one would it be?" or "Yolanda, tell us a story in which this group acts like the hero-group." Because this strategy has received relatively little attention in the applied literature, Figure 8.1 presents a sampling of other storytelling questions that can be used in schools.

Storytelling is nicely suited for use in the schools since most participants in this setting are used to telling and hearing stories (elementary children and teachers) or are not too many years away from such experiences (high school students). These questions will elicit metaphors for the important experiences that have been absorbed by the focus-group. They require the use of abductive reasoning processes. It is useful to coax analogical reasoning procedures into the discussion, since the results of these methods yield useful descriptions of patterns and redundancies rather than statements of cause or blame.

Team members can scan these stories for an understanding of the group's communication rules and typical ways of relating. As always, the team is searching for possible points of impact—those dynamics that, when sufficiently pressured, can transform the system organization into a recognizably different entity.

Positive connotation is one of the most important strategies used by successful systemic therapists. These interventionists begin with the assumption that all behavior is functional, that it serves a purpose for the system in which it is embedded. They assume that, in the past, the maintenance

Figure 8.1. Questions for Eliciting Storytelling

> What is the best story that this group has been told this year?
>
> Tell a story about the big fight in here last week but give the story a different ending than the one that really happened.
>
> If Midge and Ray were characters in a story, who would they be?
>
> Start in the middle of the Cinderella story and give it an ending that the people in this group would like a lot.
>
> Tom, start to tell a story that everybody here will add to as the story moves along.
>
> If this group were a TV show, which one would you be? Who would play which parts?
>
> If you had to live your life with this group in the middle of a story, which one would it be?
>
> Tell a story about something important that happened to this group during the past month. Hide the real facts so that we'll have to guess.
>
> Tell a story about a secret that this group has.
>
> Tell us a little story in which this group gets what it deserves.

of certain attitudes and behaviors was essential in order for group goals and needs to be fulfilled. The interventionist communicates this assumption to the family and, in doing so, finds himself or herself positively connoting the identified attitudes and behaviors. Upon first inspection, this strategy seems a bit artificial or, perhaps, manipulative. For example, a systemic family therapist might positively connote the "tantrums" of the family's youngest child by connecting them to family needs and, thus, seeing them as a service to the family. The therapist's statements might sound something like "David is the glue that holds the family together. Every time he senses that the family is in danger of coming apart he has a tantrum so that the family can focus on something and work together to try to understand it. Because of this, David's behavior is very crucial. Without it, the family might not survive." In another situation, the therapists might positively connote a young daughter's silence by viewing it as a positive event for other family members who are, themselves, afraid to speak their feelings but find they must when Jean turns so completely silent for hours at a time. She is then the one who draws the family members out of themselves. She wants the family to speak its true feelings so badly that she is willing to give up her own right to speak so that others can.

These examples illustrate in a potent way some aspects of the uniqueness of the systemic approach. If these thoughts were to be delivered by the therapists from a conventional linear mindset, they would indeed be manipulations designed solely, perhaps, for the purpose of deception of some sort. However, since positive connotation emerges from a systemic perspective, its purpose is rooted in that perspective. Positive connotation is designed to elicit differences that make a difference and to point out to the family that attitudes and behaviors are *functional* — especially where affect is involved. Behaviors that are an important part of family life occur for functional reasons. They serve the system in some important way. Evidence for this can be found as we note that these behaviors, almost always, are not found when the identified family member is participating in other groups, such as the church or school.

As they positively connote behavior, systemic therapists understand that, from one frame of reference, what they say is really quite "true." These behaviors *do* function in the identified way. The intention of the family member who exhibits this behavior is not necessarily a determinant of its function vis-a-vis the family. Some therapists, however, often add to the positive connotation the idea that the given family member has always intended that the result be a good one for the family. Those who add this perspective to the basic idea think that it enhances effectiveness. It is not necessary to include this additional thought in order for positive connotation to work. I recommend that interventionists use this variation if it is comfortable to do so; if the strategy does not devolve into a manipulative technique. Usually, the best credibility check is to ascertain the extent to which the interventionist finds genuine validity in what he or she is saying. As with any therapy, the more genuine the instance, the better for the client and the entire situation.

A by-product of this strategy is that members of the group find themselves thinking good things about themselves. Often, this occurs in the midst of situations that have been viewed as hopeless and experienced as noxious. It is not uncommon for people to dislike themselves as they function within disturbed groups. The positive connotation strategy begins a trend toward reversing such experiences. Individuals begin to see their behavior as *useful* for something, a valuable group goal or need. Valuing of self, others, and the group beings to happen.

In the schools, effective positive connotation statements serve the same purposes as within family settings. An interventionist might comment that "the antagonism Linda and Bob often show makes it possible for the whole group to get along because the antagonisms that the group has felt the need to keep secret are expressed for the group by Linda and Bob. Because of this, the group has not had to deal directly with its problems and that has served the group well in the past. Now that the team is available to help, it may not be necessary to keep the antagonisms quite so secret." In another situation, the team members may positively connote the sternness of a teacher by recognizing that sternness often emerges out of love and, since the teacher has noted that so many in the group need extra loving this year, he has decided to provide it by offering the sternness he received as a child from those who loved him.

When applying this strategy to the situation, it is crucial to realize that what one is saying is valid within the systemic perspective. If it is valid, it becomes obvious that the identified attitude and/or behavior does not need to change. It is serving an important function. I stress this because it is so easy for positive connotation to veer off into a call for change. It is not necessary to suggest change. In fact, it is counterproductive within this model to do so. Change, of course, is the metagoal — and it will occur. However, it is important to remind one another that when systemic intervention is in progress, movement comes about in a way different than what we typically expect. Change will occur when an important communication rule is identified and targeted for pressure. In systemic work, the rule is pressured, not the behavior, the person, or the group.

Positive connotation, when used effectively, functions both as a diagnostic and intervention tool. While not exclusively diagnostic, recursive questioning and storytelling are very useful strategies for eliciting the kinds of information on which intervention decisions are based. In contrast, prescriptions and rituals are strategies oriented primarily toward the direct intervention aspects of the systemic process.

Prescriptions are offered in order to acknowledge the therapeutic nature of the process, to discover the level of group commitment to the intervention, and to challenge the group's structure and methods of communication. A prescription is almost always useful when given in the first session. In most cases, others should be assigned during subsequent sessions as well. Prescriptions can be referred to in the schools as *homework*. Indeed, they function in a manner similar to academic homework, by providing initial experience or practice with new concepts. There is probably no particular advantage in most settings to referring to this activity as either a prescription or as homework. While the former term lends more solemn dignity to the experience the latter term is a more comfortable one for the school. The team should weigh the benefits of both choices for its particular setting and decide accordingly. Whatever is decided, the matter should be treated with great respect when discussing it with the focus-group. It should be made clear that success or failure — change that will feel better for everyone — *depends* upon carrying out the prescription.

The prescription is communicated to the focus-group subsequent to the meeting of the double teams after the initial contact episode. The prescription represents an attempt at identification and impact with respect to a nodal point. As a result of the contact episode, the entire team has created hypotheses as to an appropriate point of impact. The prescription is designed to further clarify the nature of that point and to begin pressuring it.

Often, the prescription can effectively build on a positive connotation that has been offered during the session. For example, the contact team will return to the room, announce that discussion with the other team has led to agreement that "the behavior of the boys during social studies, while difficult and noisy, is important for the group and should continue as is for the next 4 weeks. It is a matter of some importance that all persons in the group support this activity, since the well-being of everyone is so tied to it right now."

The intent of this strategy is to provide legitimacy for those methods that the group has been using in order for the members to coexist. It also serves to exaggerate an issue that has been associated with group discomfort. While the behaviors have been functional, they also have been unpleasant. Exaggeration of the situation, through positive sanction and prescription, provides the group with direct *access* to these behaviors. That is, something that was useful, uncomfortable, and largely unnoticed becomes available to the group. Usually, this results in an eventual modification of the practice, or it serves as a springboard to a totally new level of organization or communication.

Most positive connotations can be moved to the level of prescription. It is important that this not occur until the full team has had time to meet, make decisions, and soberly carry them back to the focus-group. It is also important to stress that the behavior must continue for the full length of time between systemic sessions.

Most effective prescriptions within the schools will require that the focus-group continue experiencing a dynamic that has been present for quite some time and is characteristically functional, uncomfortable, and largely below the level of the group's conscious awareness. Variations on the theme can result from asking the group to attend carefully to a particular aspect of the experience as it is repeated each time. Group members may be expected to comment on this aspect for a short period of time; or perhaps, silent experiencing will be all that is needed. It is important to stress that blame is to be totally absent. In fact, those who are repeating the functional and uncomfortable behaviors are providing a service to the whole group.

A specialized version of the prescription has been called the *ritual*. This strategy was originated by the Milan Associates who define it as "an action or series of actions, usually accompanied by verbal formulas or expressions, which are to be carried out by all members" of the group. The place, time, number of repetitions, specific roles and actions, and all other details of the ritual are carefully communicated by the team members. The ritual usually has a number of specific goals attached to it. These goals are not shared with the focus-group. Rather, they are constructed by the intervention team in order to help the team form hypotheses about group dynamics, structure team thinking about the issues, and introduce a potent intervention. As is the case with prescriptions in general, rituals should never be introduced lightly. The goals need to be clearly delineated. The major goal of all strategies is to instigate communication about communication. Typically, a specific goal of the ritual is to create group awareness of an issue. Another often-referenced goal is to create a situation where the group necessarily will need to experience itself as a group: an entity with a clear identity and specific membership. This second goal is particularly important for work in the schools. The focus-groups in the schools tend not to have the solid identities so typical to families. The ritual helps to form the group as a cohesive entity. A third goal often associated with the ritual is that all members of the group be provided with an opportunity to express themselves with legitimacy and without fear of interruption or other forms of harassment. Thus, most rituals provide opportunity for all members to speak, or occasionally they provide opportunity for speech only for those who are most often contradicted or put-down in some other way. It is worthwhile to consider these three goals when designing the ritual. In addition, each ritual should be the object of at least two other goals especially designed for the focus-group and situation at hand.

A ritual calls for the focus-group to repeat a specific, carefully articulated, series of actions for a specified number of times. For example, a fourth grade classroom group, which is very noisy, disruptive, and unkind to one another, might be asked to begin each Monday morning with the following ritual: The teacher and all children must utter at a normal pitch (not loud nor soft) one word that secretly describes a good quality of someone in the group. Under no circumstances is anyone ever to reveal with what person the word is associated. For exactly 12 minutes subsequent to the telling of the words, each of four persons will pick one of the words and tell why that would be a particularly good quality for a brother or sister to have. The four persons who are to speak will realize their assignment to do so as the teacher reaches into a box that contains pieces of paper put there by the intervention team. Each paper contains a statement such as "Four persons chosen by Thelma Evans who have last names that begin with a D" or "The four shortest girls in the class." The 12 minutes are to be timed by an alarm clock, which sits in the room all week but is reserved specifically for this event. When the alarm goes off, signalling the end of the speaking part of the session, all members of the group are to sit silently for an additional 3 minutes, also timed by the clock. The group members are to think about anything they want during this time. They may or may not share what they were thinking about; it is up to them. However, if they decide to share it, they may not do so until after the bell has rung for lunch break on that day. The team members will decide which four persons will be responsible for setting the alarm timing on the clock. A different person will be responsible each week and they will be named, in order, by the contact team during the session in which the ritual is prescribed. Under no circumstances is anyone to discuss the ritual, either what happens during it or anything else associated with it, at any other time. Comments will be heard only when the intervention team joins the group in 4 weeks.

The goals of this intervention ritual are:

1. To promote metacommunication.
2. To create awareness of what it is like when group members contribute in an orderly, systematic fashion.
3. To define the classroom group as a unit with its own identity, culture, and ritual.
4. To reinforce the belief that all members of the group have a right to speak and to be heard.
5. To focus attention on the pleasant personal qualities of group members. To establish recognition that such qualities are valuable.
6. To validate the right and need for quiet, personal time within the context of the group.
7. To provide opportunity for the most maligned or neglected children to play an important role. To provide opportunity for the recognition that people need to be heard even when chance, not right, has provided them the opportunity.

The first four goals are typically associated with rituals. They represent important needs for any group and especially for troubled groups. The final three goals are designed specifically for needs experienced by this particular group. A working hypothesis for this focus-group might be that an appropriate nodal point is to be found in the communication rule requiring noise rather than real conversation. That is, it may be a rule with this group that silence is never to be tolerated. The function of such a rule might be explored in a further session, especially if the ritual produces interesting movement on the part of this group.

Applicability to the Schools

All strategies are designed to encourage talking about the group's unspoken rules of communication. Rituals such as the one just described may or may not be used in addition to another form of prescription. It is wise to use only one form of prescription during the first months of an intervention, so as not to create needless confusion and to focus energy on a single nodal point. This approach is particularly useful during initial months of the intervention, when knowledge concerning an appropriate point of impact is at a minimum. When firmer conclusions have been drawn about an appropriate nodal point to focus upon, it is more likely that two prescriptions (a generic prescription and a ritual) can be effective rather than distracting.

Prescriptions in general, and rituals in particular, can be very effective with children of all ages. Younger children are particularly fascinated by rules. They love to learn them and abide by them. The rules contained within prescriptions are of natural interest for younger elementary children. We know that during the middle school years, children can be passionate about rituals and other forms of activities that dramatically contribute to group identity. In high school, students are developmentally eager to establish their identities as members of salient peer groups. Thus, these successful family strategies have natural potential for adaptation to the schools.

It was noted in an earlier chapter that the Americanized versions of systemic therapy tend to rely more heavily on dramatic personalities than do the European versions. The Milan Associates believed that systemic interventionists do not need to be charismatic. Rather, they find the technique, itself, dramatic enough that the personality of the therapist is irrelevant. In either case, it is useful to note that the concept of the dramatic moment — whether created by a person or by a method — is particularly suited to work in the schools. Children like drama. Their imaginations are responsive to the dramatic scene. This reality is fortuitous for systemic interventionists working in the schools. The lowered pitch of the voice, the mysterious pause before asking the question or assigning the prescription — these contribute to the effectiveness of the method. An interventionist who plays the game well tends to enjoy the drama of the game as well.

THE REFERRED PERSON

It is not yet common for groups rather than individuals to be referred for mental health services. In the family therapy literature, the person referred for service has been called the *identified patient*. Use of this term has helped family therapists to think of the group as the entity that needs service and the identified patient as that family member who expresses the family's symptoms in the most obvious way. While all members of the family are "patients" within this perspective, a particular individual is always *the* patient in the eyes of the family. Usually, even the identified individual accepts this label.

When a child is referred to a therapist and the therapist decides that family therapy is in order rather than individual therapy, a decision has been made that the problem is a systemic one. The situation is analogous to going to a physician with a specific complaint about a portion of your body, such as your stomach or back, only to discover that the problem is considered to be systemic rather than localized. You are not getting enough rest; you aren't eating correctly; there is too much stress in your daily life; and so forth.

The strategies I have outlined earlier fit a systemic model of intervention in the schools. Thus, they are based on a premise that an identified problem is not localized within a particular group, that the problem is not solely owned by the referred individual. This can be a legitimate way of construing school-based difficulties more often than we have realized in the past. Our conventional Western minds directed that we think in mechanistic and causal terms. This forced us to search for the broken or sick parts so that we could repair or cure them. No doubt, many of the times that we used this approach in the schools in the past, it would have been more efficacious if we had adopted a mindset that set us on a search for faulty communication patterns within important school-based groups.

Communication provides the foundation for all varieties of social behavior. When social things go "wrong," most often a faulty pattern of communication is somewhere in the picture—in the present, the past, or both. These statements represent a perspective on human behavior that we have begun to appreciate only recently. The power of the mechanistic, pathological model of behavior has probably been pushed to the limit of its usefulness. The potency of a new way of thinking about our emotional pains and discomforts is already being successfully tested in a variety of places. We know when and where the mechanistic, person-centered approach to problems will "work." We know quite a bit about that. We also have plenty of experience that shows us under what conditions it will *not* work. One of the major settings where the older way of thinking about problems has had limited success is in the public schools. Perhaps, this has been true because the schools contain systems within systems within systems. The power of a group to interrupt a person-oriented treatment plan is available at the sound of every class period bell and as the child crosses the threshold into each classroom, library, or study hall. The possibilities of working *with* the influence of the group rather than against it are compelling. The schools may be the most exciting place for the application of a systems approach to mental health.

One of the biggest tasks facing the novice systemic intervention team revolves around the decision that a referred person might best be served from within a systemic frame of reference. Some persons referred for mental health services within the schools are so much a part of cohesive groups outside the school that most attitudes and behaviors almost seem to be controlled by those systems. The influence of school-based groups is minimal in these cases. School phobia and the alienated street-based teenager come to mind. In the former case, the family system is often so strong and the communication systems so binding that the child cannot dare to leave the family system. The possibility of influence for other groups is all but absent. In the case of the street-based teenager, the system operating on the street corner functions in much the same way as the phobic child's family. The rule is "Do not join other groups. If you do, you will lose your place in this one. If that happens, you will not be able to survive."

Systemic interventionists must decide rather quickly in the referral process which cases lend themselves to systemic work and which do not. At first, more cases will seem not to fit than would seem to have applicability. These judgments will change as more experience with the method creates a greater appreciation for what it can accomplish. I recommend that cases be considered for systemic intervention when the referred person is seen by others as someone who exhibits behaviors within a group that the group experiences as uncomfortable, obnoxious, or distancing. Some of the labels often applied to the person are "stubborn, hostile, fragile, shy, withdrawn, distant, talkative, noisy, lazy, excitable, uncooperative, and unlikable." These children "cry, whine, hit, take things, break things, cling, chatter, mumble, argue, fight, and won't listen." They are "bullies, cry babies, wimps, tough-guys, show-offs, primadonnas, and princesses." Almost always, the referral will indicate that the problem is located within the child or the teacher or the administrator. It is the systemic team's job to decide that the problem can be usefully cast as one that belongs to a particular focus-group.

A good question to ask is "When this person is in the school, is he or she influenced by school-based groups? Do the groups in this school make a difference for this person?" If the answer is in the affirmative, it should be worthwhile to pursue the possibility that a focus-group intervention might best serve the situation. Surely, one of the obvious and most important advantages to systemic work is that more people are served within a limited set of resources; it is more cost-effective than individualized approaches.

It is important to remember that this model does not suggest that groups *control* behavior. There is no suggestion that the group causes an individual to withdraw or fight or talk back. Rather, the emphasis is on the communication patterns within the group and the ways in which these rules of the game shape behavior and attitudes. Analogously, it is not that the circulatory system in your body causes you to breathe or speak. Rather, the systemic patterns in your body move toward certain kinds of natural expression. Inevitably, if we were to pressure your circulatory system, change would result in your speech and breathing patterns. Systems are organic not mechanical. There is direct connection — that is, communication — among all parts. Certain subsystems modulate the flow of information from one part of the system to the others. When pressure is applied to an important connecting pattern, change ripples or reverberates throughout the entire system: all parts change; so does the whole.

It can be useful to monitor the changes in the referred person in the school throughout the life of the intervention. Such monitoring can provide information about how the intervention is affecting the system's parts. It also can provide useful feedback for the referring person, if he or she is not already somewhat conversant with things as a result of being a member of the focus-group. Beyond this type of attention, it is wise to abandon any special interest in the referred person. Such a posture makes it easier to truly adopt a systems-oriented perspective.

9

A CASE SIMULATION

By the crowd have they been broken;
By the crowd shall they be healed.

— Cody Marsh

The following case simulation is presented in order to illustrate the possibilities inherent in a systemic approach to school intervention. Within this case outline, hitches are described and responses to them are discussed.

THE SYSTEMIC INTERVENTION TEAM

The team was composed of four persons: two district level school psychologists (Sandy D. and Warren T.), one social worker (Maggie W.), and a third-grade teacher (Joelle K.). Three of these people had worked in the school system for at least 6 years; one school psychologist had been with the system for only 14 months. The pupil personnel director for the system had sanctioned the participation of the social worker and psychologists; the teacher's principal had agreed to support her participation and a substitute teacher was made available during the actual intervention sessions. One of the psychologists, the newest member of the staff, was a man; the other three team members were women. No decisions as to membership of the double teams were initially made. It had been agreed that the nature of the case would always dictate the makeup of the two teams.

PRELIMINARY PLANNING

This group agreed to meet once every 2 weeks for $1\frac{1}{2}$ hours during a 6-month period. Two other members of the school system teaching staff joined the group on an ad hoc basis. These two, fifth-grade teachers, had a moderate level of interest in the systemic approach and attended most of the meetings. It was agreed that they might serve as back-up team members if a situation arose that needed them. Beyond that, they agreed to assist various interventions by continuing to discuss the issues with the team members on an ad hoc basis. As a result of their involvement, both teachers began to use systemic thinking in modified versions within their classes.

The group of six persons began to meet on a regular basis in November. As a result of holidays and a particularly severe flu season, the 24 meetings were not completed until June. A relatively systematic look at the literature formed the basis of most group meetings; each important topic was assigned for consideration at a specific meeting. It had been planned that, around February, the discussions would turn to considerations peculiar to the particular school system in which these people worked. However, discussions of the applic..bility of the perspective and strategies to the local situation seemed to occur quite frequently from the very first meeting. Therefore, it was decided to incorporate this topic naturally into each session.

Initial efforts to locate a consultant were not fruitful. The group agreed not to begin a systemic intervention until a consultant could be found. During the summer break, Jim Z., a psychologist trained in school and clinical work was located in a nearby city. He was employed in a community mental health center and occasionally engaged in family therapy. He had been part of a systemic therapy team during his doctoral training program and was very interested in expanding his knowledge of systemic work. A consultant fee was agreed upon. The school district (PPS Department) consented to pay half the fee while the four team members split the cost of the remaining half. The consultant agreed to meet with the team for 1 hour each month, and as needed throughout an intervention. The team planned to meet with the consultant during the week immediately preceding an intervention session with the focus-group. The group met as a team in August in order to freshen systemic modes of thinking and plan for the coming year.

THE REFERRAL

Several promising referrals were available for team discussion during September. Choosing an appropriate initial case proved to be more difficult than anticipated. Understandably, after almost a year's preparation, the team was enthusiastic about getting started. Recognizing this, more than a moderate amount of confusion seemed to enter the picture as they culled through the available referrals. A legitimate question seemed to center on whether a given case constituted an appropriate starting point or whether the team's desire to begin quickly might be coloring their judgment in the matter. Preliminary fears that most referring issues would sound so person-centered that the cases would seem inadvisable were largely unfounded. The team inspected possible cases for evidence that the referring child or situation contained many behaviors that could legitimately be influenced by a group. Team members often asked themselves if a particular behavior might be part of an interesting communication pattern among members of a classroom or support group. Many referrals were rejected for systemic intervention because the influence of the family group seemed too salient. It was decided that this criterion was not necessary, but that chances of success with the initial case might be maximized if the referring situation did not seem to have direct connection to family dynamics rather than school dynamics.

In early October, the senior psychologist was handed a referral by the school secretary as she was leaving the largest elementary school in the system. (This was not the school in which Joelle, the third-grade teacher, worked.) Hawthorne Elementary School contained 600 children in grades kindergarten through six. The principal, Mr. Scanlan, had been associated with the school for 15 years; he was seen by most to be easygoing, yet firm. He tended to use his sense of humor in most situations. He preferred to react to the majority of problems as if they were "cute" or "silly" rather than serious. Parent groups usually approved of his decisions. His teachers felt he was supportive. The zealous loyalty of his office staff had been the object of systemwide jokes for some years. Children rarely reported either liking or disliking him. Hawthorne was one of those schools that felt comfortable upon entry. Children's work usually decorated the well-lit halls. Noise and disruption were heard only during break times.

The referral was signed by a fifth-grade teacher, who asked for psychological evaluation of a boy who had been a member of the community all his life. The referral indicated that according to records he had started "acting out" in the fourth grade and that, during the first 5 months of the present school year, he had managed to alienate every girl in the class by "accidentally" pushing them or stepping on their feet. His friends (all boys) encouraged him in these activities. Remarks from the teacher went unheeded. In fact, he seemed to increase his "hostile" behavior on the days she spoke sternly to him. The situation had come to a head 2 days previously, when he spilled paint on one of the girls, ruining her blouse and slacks. He refused to apologize, saying that it had been an accident. The girl in question came into the room the following day, marched over to him, and belted him in the stomach. In the final paragraph of the rather lengthy, written description of the problem, the teacher, Cindy Norbert, noted that she had read about a seriously disturbed "foot stomper" who was psychiatrically diagnosed as having a deep-seated hatred for women. She wondered if Paul R., the referred child, might be in the beginning stages of such a problem.

The senior psychologist, Sandy, called the other members of the team. The case sounded promising. The team members agreed simply to acknowledge their desire to "get going with this thing" and look into the Paul R. case as quickly as possible. The social worker, Maggie, contacted the principal; Sandy went to the teacher. Information was received from these sources in typical linear fashion. It seems that the parents of this boy had been divorced 3 years earlier; the parents shared custody of the child on a year-to-year basis. This school year, the boy lived with his father. He had been in his mother's custody during the fourth-grade year, and the switch had been made in midsummer. Paul was an "O.K." student. He tended to complete assignments on time, although there was some indication that he might be moving toward irresponsibility in this area; a recent math homework assignment had been 2 days late. Most of the time, he was a popular child; friendly and jovial. His school records indicated that, since first grade, he had been considered a leader in his classes. He was physically muscular and could excel in competitive sports when he put energy into that. He did not seem to be interested in sports quite as much as other boys in the class. His teacher noted that his "abuse" of the girls now was occurring on a daily basis. Other boys in the class were beginning to imitate his behavior. Ms. Norbert had asked the principal to talk to the boy, but he had suggested a psychological referral instead. Routine referral procedures had been followed. These included a phone call to the boy's parent, who sanctioned the plan and agreed to drop by the school on the way to work to sign a referral form.

The principal agreed to consider the possibility of using a systemic team approach with this case. He heard, of course, that such a team had been in preparation last year. It would be fine to try a new approach in his school. He reported that he had always enjoyed success when trying out innovative ideas.

Mr. Scanlan noted that this particular teacher was relatively new, only 3 years out of college. He did not think she was quite assertive enough with the fifth graders and wondered why she had not prepared to teach the younger elementary grades. It was not his style as an administrator to intervene in discipline matters within the classrooms unless an emergency arose. He expected his teachers to handle their own discipline. Therefore, he had asked Ms. Norbert to refer to psychological services in the hopes that the psychologist could "work wonders" with her, as she had done with another teacher last year. He would help in any way he could. Ms. Norbert could be a good teacher if only she would "get more authoritative." He commented on her short and slim stature and the softness of her voice. He had found that these characteristics did not work well with fourth, fifth, and sixth-grade kids. He was mildly opposed to the transfer of this teacher to his school 2 years ago, but he had owed the Beechwood School principal a big transfer favor and had to pay up. Personally, he liked Cindy Norbert a lot. She added a lot of youthful enthusiasm to his teaching staff, which had been pretty stable the past few years and was aging. As far as the boy was concerned, he wondered if this wasn't just another product-of-divorce case. Some acting out has to be expected in these cases, and Paul was just at the right age to tease the girls. Boys like to gain stature from that kind of thing at his age. He honestly didn't think the child was the problem here.

During the half hour that the psychologist was talking with the principal, Paul R. used his closed fist to punch a girl classmate in the stomach as she walked by his desk. The girl had difficulty catching her breath and spent the afternoon looking pale and ill. The teacher loudly reprimanded Paul and forced him to sit at the back of the classroom for the remainder of the afternoon. At the close of the day, the teacher called the psychologist to report the incident. Upon learning that the principal had not yet been informed, the psychologist suggested that be done. The teacher agreed. First, she called the boy's father, who was not yet at home. She reached him later in the evening. He seemed angry and upset over the matter and said he would punish the child. Ms. Norbert called the injured girl's parents to see how she was. Apparently, she was doing well. The teacher told the parents that she would try to assure that such a thing never happened again.

The social worker, Maggie, called the gym teacher for information. Warren dropped by to consult with the school secretary, a woman who had worked in that school even before Mr. Scanlan became principal. These consultations corroborated the facts of the story. In addition, it was noted by the secretary that the principal was getting more and more frustrated with Cindy Norbert these days, and it was rumored that Paul's mother was living with an unemployed musician who did not like the boy. The physical education teacher said that Paul didn't seem to like competitive sports although he was pretty good at them. He wondered if Paul's excess energy might not be drained off if he went out for the sixth grade football team next year.

A Systemic Look at the Referring Issues

The team decided that the Paul R. case was suited for systemic work since it (a) involved several members of (b) an intact group and (c) was located within a school that was stable and initially supportive. Other considerations were that no member of the intervention team had transactions with the group on a regular basis in other roles and that family dynamics, while important, did not preclude the possibility that classroom dynamics were of sufficient potency. Thus, Ms. Norbert's fifth-grade class became the focus-group for the intervention. It was decided that the principal, Mr. Scanlan, was not a natural member of this organic unit. Therefore, he was considered throughout the life of the intervention as administrator of the next larger system of which the focus-group was a part; his personal characteristics were considered from time to time, when the team focused on him as an individual rather than a member of the larger system. Focus-group membership became an issue at this point. Ms. Norbert agreed to participate in a systemic intervention and worked with two of the team members in identifying the names and group roles of those in the class. All students in the group were typically present and participating. Therefore, there seemed no need to plan for any special contingency regarding membership in this focus-group.

As the team met for discussion, focus was shifted away from Paul R. and to the classroom group. The case was renamed the #101 case, since this was the classroom number. It was assumed that Paul's behavior represented a symptom of the whole group's distress. The team members began to form preliminary hypotheses concerning important communication patterns. Rules relating to leadership within the group seemed to be important; a clear understanding of the processes involved was not possible at that point.

The team decided that communication processes within the focus-group might be embedded within a set of communication dynamics that could be seen within the larger system, the school. In some ways, it seemed possible that the leadership and initiative issues in the classroom might reflect the leadership issues in the school. Evidence for this seemed to be present in a pattern of communication in the school that found responsibility for problems to be in perpetual oscillation between the central office and other parts of the system. In the beginning, the team pictured a hot potato as they thought about responsibility for the Paul R. situation oscillating from principal to Cindy and back again. The rules of this game were unclear but intriguing. Somewhat reluctantly, the team concluded that the dynamics of the larger system were not at issue within this intervention. The classroom would constitute the focus-group, so consideration of the communication patterns of the larger system needed to receive reduced attention. While the team was somewhat uneasy about abandoning their interest in issues pertinent to the larger system, they, nonetheless, bound themselves to do so.

Returning conceptually to the issue of leadership in the classroom, the team devoted time to speculation concerning the manner in which rules were communicated in this group. No clearcut hypotheses could be formed. The team assumed that an intervention episode was necessary before further diagnosis could be effective. Team members continually reminded one another that the term *diagnosis* need not have causal connotations. Subsequent to meeting with the consultant, the team decided that Ms. Norbert needed to be informed of systemic intervention perspectives in as brief a fashion as possible. The team met with her for 20 minutes and carried out the plan they devised with the consultant. Ms. Norbert was told the "truth." That is, she was informed that the team intended to use a new set of techniques with this referral problem. The team looked forward to working with her classroom as a closely knit whole and, therefore, the goals of the strategies would be shared with her in the same way and at the same time that they would be shared with the rest of the group. Thus, she could expect to be "in the dark" as much as the students. It was important that she understand that her tasks were to follow any assignments as carefully as she could and, particularly, to *enjoy* the process as much as possible. Any additional support she might need should be received from the principal since, once the intervention began, the team could not discuss the particulars with her until the close of the entire effort. She could be assured that at the end of the school year, after 7 sessions spaced at monthly intervals, she would receive a complete and detailed debriefing. Her willingness to engage in this effort was ascertained. If Ms. Norbert had indicated reluctance, the team was prepared to meet again to devise another method of approaching her. Since she seemed fairly comfortable with the plan, for whatever reasons, it was decided that the intervention could officially begin. A version of the presentation to Ms. Norbert was given to the principal, who agreed to support his teacher if confusion should predominate. Mr. Scanlan agreed to "live with" as little information as the team felt the need to give him over the course of the year. Team members felt that the somewhat disjointed nature of his agreement to this part of the plan indicated that the issue of building leadership patterns had somehow been touched upon again. The team decided that Mr. Scanlan's support and involvement would need to be reprocessed throughout the life of the intervention. For the moment, the team decided to move forward with what they viewed as somewhat tentative agreement from the principal. It was later discovered that the principal had contacted the director of pupil personnel services, in order to gain her commitment to be partially responsible for the outcome of "this new psychology thing." The assurance was forthcoming and the team added this piece of information to the growing supply of data, which seemed to suggest that rules concerning leadership/responsibility were central for communication patterns at the school level, and perhaps at the system level as well. The team credited their newly emerging ability to think in terms of communication rules to the practice they were getting in scanning situations as if they were motion pictures. They searched for themes that seemed to roll around the picture from time to time and tried to think in terms of analogies as much as possible.

PLANNING FOR THE INTERVENTION

During the meeting with the consultant, the team decided primarily to orient strategies toward acquiring information concerning the rules that governed authority and leadership within the focus-group. A secondary issue was related to the communication patterns between boys and girls in this group. Thus, the team decided to use recursive questioning and storytelling techniques, in an effort to encourage the rules to become manifest.

It was decided that Maggie and Warren would work as the contact team while Sandy and Joelle would play the part of the Greek chorus. Because Joelle taught in another school, she seemed ideally suited for the out-of-room team, since it would function as the final arbiter of relevant reality for the group. Her position as a member of the school system, geographically removed from the contact group, seemed potentially helpful. A man's presence was desired on the contact team and Sandy, the senior psychologist, had been in professional contact with two of the children from this classroom within the past year. For these reasons, it was decided that Warren and Maggie would form the direct-contact team.

Since 101 was an intact classroom, it was possible to arrange for access to the group for an entire afternoon. Ms. Norbert was informed that 3 hours would be needed, but she was not told how the time would be spent. She was asked to prepare the class in any way she saw fit but to ignore the fact that Paul R.'s behavior had stimulated her request for help. The team did not question her concerning her approach to the children. As much as possible, the team intended to work with the focus-group as a whole and to keep contact with individuals at a minimum. Therefore, Ms. Norbert's status as teacher of the group was to become important only as the focus-group made it important. The team decided to accord little formal recognition to the teacher role during intervention sessions.

THE INTERVENTION SESSION

The contact team entered the room, identified themselves, and indicated that they were there to help the group function more smoothly and happily—if that were possible. The team did not know much about the functioning of the group. It was possible that it was already quite a happy and smoothly functioning group or, perhaps, it was so miserable and disorganized that it would be impossible for things to change.

The team explained that they would talk with the group for 1 hour and 20 minutes and that, at the end of that time, they would leave the room to discuss matters between themselves and with two other people, who were part of their team but did not wish to join them in the classroom. Those out of the room were described as very wise persons, who understood things quickly and sometimes almost magically. It was mentioned that these two were both women, very nice women who often were asked for their advice and opinions. These women had important jobs elsewhere in the school system. Their names were mentioned as the contact team indicated that the persons outside the room knew something about this class and might interrupt from time to time in order to find out what was going on and offer their wise counsel. It was also mentioned that if either or both of the contact persons needed to consult with those outside the room, a brief intermission would be called. The group was told that, after discussing things with the out-of-room people following the 1 hour and 20 minute session, the contact team would return to the room to tell the group what had been decided and offer suggestions. It was also mentioned that the team would contract to offer a session such as this one once every month until May.

The contact team asked if the members of this group felt like a group. If so, why? If not, why not? During this discussion the team announced, after a 10-second pause, that the group of four (those in and those outside the room) had named this the 101 group and would continue to call it that until the end of the school year. This portion of the discussion lasted 15 minutes.

The team then asked the following recursive question: "If this whole group, as a group, were to become the president of the United States, how would it perform: how would it go about getting the job done?" While that particular question had been designed during the intervention planning session, responses to it suggested additional recursive questions, which the team asked from time to time as the discussion began to unfold. For example, pushing the leadership/authority issue further, Warren asked, "What things do the older and younger persons in this group have in common when they have to make difficult decisions or when they have to do things that others won't like?" Maggie asked if "the 101 group would rather have everything given to them (including lots of money) or would they rather do everything themselves (thereby becoming famous)."

The secondary issue of girl-boy relational patterns was addressed by asking, "If a new student entered the class tomorrow would the student want to be a boy or girl? Is it better to be a girl or boy in group 101?" Since the response to this question contained more enthusiasm than any other to that time, discussion of the issue ran free for awhile and no other questions were asked by the contact team members. They supported, listened actively, and encouraged in typical helping profession style as group members expressed themselves. Special attention was paid to including Ms. Norbert as simply another member of the 101 group. At a prearranged time, there was a knock at the door. Maggie answered the door, announced dramatically that the out-of-room people were summoning her, and Warren continued the discussion in progress for 4 minutes. During the fifth and sixth minutes, he raised his hand to stop conversation, became silent, and looked toward the door with an anxious expression on his face. (This emotion validly portrayed his true feelings since he personally disliked standing silently in front of a group—any group.) As prearranged, exactly 6 minutes after the leaving of the room, Maggie appeared, stating that she had innocently described what had been going on thus far: "a fun conversation with a great group." To her surprise, these people said they absolutely knew of things that the contact team could only guess at. They demanded that the group stop what it was doing and make up a story that answered the following question: "If all of the boys in the room suddenly became one fifth-grade boy, named Chip, and all the girls (including Cindy Norbert) magically became one fifth-grade girl, named Allison, what would Allison and Chip do if they were trapped on an island by a strange person who made up all the rules and had all the power but hid from Chip and Allison so they never could find that person for confrontation?"

Intersession Planning

The four team members came together for 1 hour following the contact episode. Immediately, the out-of-room team began to question the contact team concerning what had transpired. They used systemic questions so that the report would not contain causal statements or depend upon linear thinking. Often, the out-of-room team employed recursive questioning in order to elicit information. They talked to the contact team as if Maggie and Warren were members of the 101 group. For example, the contact team was asked, "When you two were in the room, how did Warren fit with the boys and how did Maggie fit with the girls? And, what were the cross-sex similarities? What were the points of connection between Maggie and the boys and Warren and the girls?"

Since the Greek chorus could not observe the action through use of a one-way mirror, this method of eliciting description had to substitute for the conventional one-way mirror observation associated with systemic family therapy. While recognizing the limitations of this modified procedure for producing a picture of the contact episode, the team, nonetheless, felt that it adequately served its purpose. For example, occasionally, initial responses to the questions were heavily linear and, overall, it was obvious that the contact team had become enmeshed in the dynamics of the focus-group. They tended to feel hopeless about certain things and suffered a tendency to want to blame particular members of the group. As a result, this portion of the intrasession planning time stretched to 30 minutes, and Warren had to tell the focus-group that the team would be precisely 15 minutes late returning to them, because something interesting had come up which needed very thorough attention prior to a sharing with 101. As a result of the "regrounding" portion of the planning session, the contact team could eventually return to systemic perspectives concerning what had occurred within the classroom. Thus, the group could begin to identify possible nodal points and prescription strategies. It was decided that the pattern in which girls and boys were treated very differently in 101 could constitute an important communication dynamic for the group. Within the systemic frame of reference, it became clear that neither Ms. Norbert nor any other person was responsible for the origination and maintenance of this rule. Discomfort seemed to arise from it; yet, it seemed functional for creating a "group feeling" and, even, for helping to accomplish the daily tasks within the classroom. The team began to guess that the issue of authority and group leadership was embedded somewhere within the complicated pattern of rules governing what girls could do and what boys could do in 101. Therefore, as a way of providing for further diagnostic information and as a way of beginning the formal intervention aspects of the procedure, the team designed a prescription that might impact on the communication patterns of interest.

The Prescription

Playing upon the drama created by the reported reactions of the Greek chorus, the team designed a ritual prescription for the group. The contact team rejoined the focus-group at precisely the stated moment and announced that those outside the room had offered a startling collection of opinions and suggestions. For one thing, the out-of-room people thought it was possible that Maggie and Warren had become too close to the group. They were not sure, but thought it was possible. At any rate, they had suggested something that needed to be done in this group and, since the contact team had never — repeat, never — known them to be wrong about these matters, they were going to support the suggestion wholeheartedly, even though they did not fully understand its benefits. The contact team reported their eagerness to experiment with this very new way of thinking about problems. They only wished that they could be around to join 101 as they accomplished the assigned task. Of course, that could not be possible, since they were not really a part of 101, only visitors. It was important that the group be aware that the task was designed *only* for use by 101 and would never be used by anyone else.

The 101 group was told that twice each week, on Monday and Thursday, at exactly 9:10 in the morning, the group was to stop what it was doing. It was important that the group not plan a morning lesson that would end just before 9:10; rather, the group must *interrupt* an activity. John G. would give the stop signal on the first two Mondays while Becky M. was to give the signal on the first two Thursdays. Both Becky and John were to give the signal together on Mondays and Thursdays during the last two weeks of the months. (That Becky and John had been seen as group leaders, who were somewhat low-key, was not shared with the group.) The signal would be that the person or persons assigned the stop signal would march, not walk, to the front of the room at exactly 9:10 and loudly say, "101 will now regroup!" The members of the group were to sit comfortably in their chairs (that is, they were to adopt whatever body posture felt the best to them) and were to face the front of the room. During the first week, on both Monday and Thursday, Kay F. (the girl who was punched) was to move slowly but deliberately to the corner of the room where the contact team members would put a very special black box which would contain a message for 101. Each time the ritual occurred, there would be only one message in the box. During the first week, Kay was to reach her hand into the box, draw out the message and read it slowly and loudly to the group twice. Washington C. and Carrie N. were to do this during the second and third weeks, respectively. Paul R. was to do it during the fourth, and final, week. The message contained in the box would tell the group a special thing to do. It must be done exactly as described and was to last no more than 18 minutes. The person pulling the message from the box was to time the activity on the classroom clock. He or would say "begin" as soon as the message was read the second time and would say "stop" exactly 18 minutes later. No matter how strange the message, it was important that it be followed exactly. Absolutely nothing else was to go on from the time the stop signal began until the person said "stop," at the close of the 18 minute period: no talking, no getting up, nothing but what the message required. The ritual was not to be discussed outside the class with anyone else in the school. This ritual belonged *only* to 101.

The contact team repeated these instructions twice, then asked for a volunteer to repeat the instructions a third time. A girl was chosen to do this. After she was finished, a boy was called on to assist her with the wording of the final step in the process. Subsequently, the team members stood up quite straight at the front of the room, raised their fingers to their lips in a gesture of silence, stared thoughtfully at the group for exactly 15 seconds, turned to one another then back to the group, as each said quite solemnly, "good luck." Then, they walked from the room.

The purposes of this ritual were the following:

1. to encourage metacommunication
2. to help the group solidify as a unit
3. to give experience in systematic turn taking
4. to reinforce the belief that all members have the right to speak and be heard
5. to provide opportunities for both girls and boys to play legitimate authority roles
6. to provide experience for boys and girls to share together and act together
7. to provide experience for systematic participation in leadership roles

Post-Episode Planning

During post-episode planning, the team created eight messages and made arrangements for them to be tucked into the box prior to the group's arrival on Monday and Thursday mornings. Creating the messages took much longer than anticipated and, thus, it was necessary for the team to meet again after school the following day when post-episode debriefing occurred at greater length. As an example of the kind of prescription placed in the box, the first message read that each person in the group was to notice one article of clothing worn by the person directly in front of him or her. Beginning with the person nearest the front window, each person would mention the name of the person and the article of clothing. Those sitting in the front seat were to mention an article of clothing worn by Ms. Norbert who, for her part, would comment in turn on the person sitting directly in front of her. Each person was to choose the clothing article they liked the very best. The name and the article should be said loudly with exactly a 2-second pause separating them. At the end of the message, there was a note that told the group that discussion of this message or any of the messages to come (or the ritual, in general) could occur with only one other person in class. In order that there be no confusion about this, each person in the class had been paired with another and the list of pairs would now be read by Kay F. (Each pair contained a boy and a girl.) The members of 101 did not *have* to discuss any part of the ritual. However, since Maggie and Warren knew that this group was very good at discussing and enjoyed it, they had convinced the out-of-room people to allow this small deviation from secrecy and silence. It could be used throughout the month if the members of 101 wanted to do so. The note reminded that only within the assigned pairs could persons discuss what happened during the next 4 weeks during the 101 ritual time.

During the 4-week period, another message called for pairing of group members. Within that particular one, Kay F. and Paul R. were paired. This message was the very last one given.

During the post-session debriefing following the first session, the contact team realized that they had not told the focus-group exactly when they would be back for a second visit. Therefore, they appended this piece of information to the second message. The team also opined to themselves that they had decided to provide the group with eight messages. In a sense, they were producing eight different prescriptions — an effective strategy, but an unnecessary one that had become costly in terms of team time. Further hypotheses also were produced at this meeting and the group settled on a time to meet with Jim Z., the consultant, prior to the next intervention session.

SUBSEQUENT INTERVENTION SESSIONS

Team members smiled supportively and pleasantly to Ms. Norbert and other group members when passing them in the halls or at a local grocery store or gas station. No words were ever spoken to group members outside of intervention sessions.

A similar format was followed during all sessions. In all, four rituals were assigned and three generic prescriptions across the life of the intervention. In January, one important prescription called for the student members of the group to address Ms. Norbert as Cynthia (not Cindy) each Tuesday for 4 weeks. There were two additional parts to that prescription, which had been based on the team's desire to begin establishing more clearly Ms. Norbert's credentials as titular and substantive head of the group. This strategy proved to be among the most effective used. Storytelling was heavily relied upon.

During the middle of the 7-month cycle, the team moved away from searching for a point of impact that involved boy-girl communication patterns. They concentrated solely on leadership and authority issues. The goal was not to produce change; rather, the goal was to help the rules already present to become clear. During the final intervention session, the girl-boy issue was raised again and a part of the prescription was geared toward it. Since the group would not be meeting with 101 at the end of the last 4-week period, the contact team suggested that the group schedule their own last ritual meeting and that Ms. Norbert be in charge of designing an appropriate task, whose purpose simply would be that the group have an "awful lot of fun."

The role of the Greek chorus waxed and waned over the course of the intervention. That team was put to good use when debriefing and understanding were needed; however, that team's relation to the focus group was never fully "perfected." The team decided that they were not as proficient in using the out-of-room team as they would like to be. Occasionally, they balked at making the out-of-room team appear to be the "villains," since they were afraid of negative parental feedback aimed at the members of that team. When processing this intervention, the group decided that their concerns had been ill-founded with this particular focus-group since, from the beginning, the group as a whole had enjoyed the drama of it all and, in general, had few complaints. In addition, the "villain" analogy had not proved a good one and had, perhaps, influenced their own responses to the out-of-room team. During a March meeting, 101 had complained a bit about the contact team and the out-of-room team as well; however, the team concluded that this was a manifestation of strengthened bonds within the group. It was decided that with future cases, the authority-figure aspect of the out-of-room team would be de-emphasized only when hostility toward authority figures seemed to be one of the behavioral dynamics in the communication rules for a particular group. With continued team experience, even that contingency might constitute an appropriate use of the Greek chorus version of the out-of-room team. The team also decided to create a "benevolence" role for the Greek chorus that would be available for balancing an authority role.

Case Conclusion

By May, the final month of the 7-session intervention, it had become obvious that the 101 group had shifted in several important ways. The group thought of itself as the "best" group in the school, one that "took care of its own problems" and "helped when a 101 kid needed help." Communication patterns between boys and girls seemed to be more open, although it was not uncommon for members of the group to be heard weighing the various merits of being one gender or the other. Pushing, punching, and fighting occurred within the group no more often than it did in the other fifth-grade classrooms at Hawthorne. The group had learned to "settle down" quickly at the sight or sound of a cue for quiet, but it occasionally became somewhat unruly when a spirited class discussion was in progress. During the life of the intervention, it had become more difficult for people to systematically take turns speaking during an interesting discussion. The group found no satisfactory solution to the problems this created. In general, the group was proud of itself. It thought of itself as unique. Importantly, it often seemed willing to accept the "faults" of its members.

There were several obvious changes in specific members of the group. By the end of the year, three formerly shy and reticent people seemed to enjoy participation in discussions. Paul R.'s pushing and punching lessened considerably and when they did occur, they were directed equally toward boys and girls. Ms. Norbert seemed to have changed very little; that is, her responses to the group and the stimuli she offered as a teacher seemed to remain pretty much as they were at the beginning of the intervention. The team remained puzzled about this phenomenon. For a while, their favored hypothesis was that the group had learned to accommodate Ms. Norbert, to achieve group goals in spite of her. Finally, the team became frustrated with itself, as it realized that this construction of the situation was quite linear. The team had assumed that Ms. Norbert needed changing and that if this change did not occur then obviously the class must have changed toward her. Realizing the problem, the team eventually decided that, perhaps, it had not observed the situation carefully enough. Indeed, relatively little attention had been paid to the teacher's behavior in the beginning, since the focus was on the group. In addition, it was quite possible that when the team decided that Ms. Norbert had not changed, perhaps they meant that she had not changed toward the team, the principal, and her role in the school. The team acknowledged that they knew very little about the context of Ms. Norbert's involvement with the focus-group or the dynamics of any changes that may have occurred for her. Since she agreed with the team and the principal that the intervention had been successful, there seemed to be no point in further conjecture on the matter.

All major parties to the intervention agreed that it had been effective. All admitted that they had been anxious over it initially and at other confusing points throughout the process. However, the principal was eager that his school receive this type of service in the future.

One of the biggest problems faced by the team at the end of the year was the continual stream of questions concerning this new intervention from other parts of the system. People in all the schools seemed to have heard about it. Some wanted to see it operate in their school, classroom, or special education group. Others expressed distrust and concern. Those at Hawthorne had the fewest problems in this area. Their principal noted that nothing could be reported about what was going on with Ms. Norbert's class; therefore, they did not ask questions. The team scheduled a meeting for midsummer to review the intervention and plan for the following year. They decided that first on the agenda would be the issue of what to say to interested parties in other parts of the system, since each member of the team believed that he or she had done a poor job of fielding such questions. The second item of business concerned the errors that team members had made. Maggie and Warren had continually thought their pacing was either too fast or too slow. Joelle and Sandy had not been able to apprehend quickly enough what had been going on in the classroom during contact episodes. The out-of-room team needed to develop better ways to make up for the lack of a one-way mirror and the limits on perception that created.

The team concluded that it had been most successful in using abductive reasoning and the storytelling technique, as well as devising effective prescriptions that were not unduly risky.

The last comment, made as the team was ending its final meeting of the year, was directed toward an important dynamic within the larger system. The team noted that if they had not been supported by people in other parts of the system (such as the PPS director, Hawthorne's secretary, and an assistant superintendent), the intervention might have been much less successful.

10

OTHER APPROACHES TO SYSTEMS PSYCHOLOGY IN THE SCHOOLS

Daring ideas are like chessmen moved forward; they may be beaten, but they may start a winning game.
— Johann Wolfgang von Goethe

Several promising examples of approaches to the practice of psychology in the schools are systems-oriented but different from the systemic version. In general, these methods do not require as radical a departure from traditional modes of contemporary Western thought. Thus, in varying degrees, each of them relies on conventional ways of thinking about causality. What distinguishes these perspectives from older ways of looking at problems is that they see the system as controlling the development of attitudes and behaviors. The focus is on the group rather than on an individual. Often, these approaches emphasize multiple causes rather than single causes. Several of these models will be categorized and outlined in this chapter. The final model mentioned is complementary to the one described at length in this volume, since it is partially indebted to the thinking of the Milan family therapists.

ECOSYSTEMIC APPROACHES

Lusterman (1985) thinks of an ecosystemic approach as one that conceptualizes a given system as a subsystem within a larger system. For example, in certain contexts, he finds it useful to think of a family as a system that is part of another system, such as the school. Within his approach, the psychologist or social worker places himself or herself at the interface between the school system and family system.

Lusterman recommends using this model in cases where discord between home and school has arisen. Both school and family are given a statement entitled, *Tension Between School and Family*. The document discusses home-school relations in general terms and notes that when tensions have been prolonged, it is sometimes useful to cut off contact between the two groups. The following steps represent abbreviated versions of the suggestions found in the document (Lusterman, 1985, p. 25):

1. Complete disengagement: The family therapist separates out the home problems from the school problems. . . .
2. The therapist contracts an agreement . . . that [the school] will contact the therapist [when problems arise]. The family agrees to a temporary hands-off policy.
3. The therapist works with the family to correct non-school-related problems.
4. As the therapist sees some improvement in the home situation, she/he gradually reintroduces parent-school involvement. . . .
5. The therapist withdraws as more appropriate and productive contact between school and family is established.

The mental health worker uses the messages received from the school and family to map patterns of communication that have been preventing a solution to the problem. Within the Lusterman model, the psychologist or social worker acts as "a temporary buffer zone."

Obviously, the practitioner accepts a great deal of responsibility within this model. He or she becomes the channel through which all communication flows. The approach provides a hands-on-method of directly changing communication patterns.

Aponte (1976) describes an ecostructural approach that focuses attention on four levels of interest: the individual, the family, the school, and the social context. He is concerned with the structures of these systems and the dynamics that give them life. Within the spirit of all systems orientations, Aponte notes that, "a boy having trouble in school is not having trouble alone." Nonetheless, the Aponte approach accords the child attention in a very traditional way. His or her history and personality characteristics are taken into account and conceptually related to the family, which is construed as the second context for the child's "being and becoming." Within the school, persons important to the referred child are interviewed. Finally, sociocultural influences are considered. The referred child remains the focus of attention at all times. The character of the system under scrutiny is not as important as its relation to the child. The practitioner targets all systems as the intervention proceeds. Important representatives from these systems are invited to a meeting, where the referred child is also present. Aponte describes techniques for assessing communication patterns between the child and all other systems. Occasionally, during this meeting, the practitioner deliberately connects with the child in an effort to dislodge old habits of "using" the child in maladaptive ways.

Both Lusterman and Aponte are concerned with the interfaces between and among systems that are crucial to the life of the child. Both approaches use the practitioner in a direct and authoritative way, seeking to employ him or her as the instrument that produces change.

Another similar ecosystemic approach has been described by Tittler and Cook (1981), who also convene a meeting of representatives from all the systems important to the child. Unlike the Lusterman and Aponte approaches, however, the Tittler and Cook approach calls for the practitioner to function more as facilitator than leader. The intent is to form a version of a group identity by allowing the individuals present to work toward an intervention plan that makes sense to all concerned. Thus, this systems approach demands less responsibility on the part of the mental health worker. It more quickly shifts responsibility to the various salient actors and actresses in the child's life.

THE LIAISON FUNCTION

In the early 1960s, Nicholas Hobbs (1966; 1975; Hobbs et al., 1979) developed a vision for re-educating children thought of as severely emotionally disturbed. While he believed that these children could best be served within a residential environment, he rejected the traditional notion that troubled children needed total separation from their troubled families. Therefore, the programs he developed called for frequent in-home contact, often for an entire weekend.

Hobbs was determined to provide environments for children that emphasized education and strength rather than pathology. Today, there are over 20 Project Re-Ed schools operating within the Hobbs philosophy. Early in the process of Re-Ed development, he wrote

> We assume that the child is an inseparable part of a small social system, of an ecological unit made up of the child, his family, his school, his neighborhood and community. . . . The effort is to get each component of the system above threshold with respect to the requirements of the other components. The Re-Ed school becomes a part of the ecological unit for as brief a period of time as possible, withdrawing when the probability that the system will function appears to exceed the probability that it will not. We used to speak of putting the child back into the system but we have come to recognize the erroneous assumption involved; the child defines the system and all we can do is withdraw from it at a propitious moment. (Hobbs, 1966, p. 1108)

Embedded within the liaison approach is the role of liaison professional. Hobbs thought of the liaison specialist as one who crosses the boundaries among systems, assessing strengths and mobilizing resources prior to educating adults and children in liaison strategies, so that they may take over these important functions as the specialist withdraws. The liaison interventionist is concerned with linkages. He or she reorders energies within a system so that it capitalizes on its own strengths. An intervention strategy based on an appreciation of the liaison function was developed by Dokecki (1977), Newbrough (1977a), and Williams (1977) for use within community psychology.

A few years ago, with intellectual indebtedness to those cited above, I described a public school-based adaptation of the liaison approach (Plas, 1981). The method is grounded in ecological, transactional, and systems theory and is directed by seven theoretical biases:

1. The child exists within an ecology. All events are a function of the person-environment process. Thus, problems and possibilities for change do not reside exclusively within individuals.
2. Rather than cause-effect interactions, the liaison psychologist seeks to identify and influence relationships within a unified whole.
3. The whole is something more than the sum of its parts.
4. The "reality" of a situation is a function of the observer's position relative to that which is observed.
5. The dynamic processes involved in growth and change are the phenomena best suited to assessment and intervention.
6. The intervention process must capitalize on strengths.
7. Synergic system energy should be important within the change process.

Only the seventh of these should be unfamiliar to the reader at this point. *Synergy* is defined by Craig and Craig (1974) as "the working together of unlike elements to create desirable results unobtainable from any combination of independent events" (p. 62). Synergic power is related to the *differences* people experience among themselves. Within the constellation of differences peculiar to any problematic situation, there resides the potential for creation, for positive change. As I commented elsewhere

> Within more traditional approaches, once a "problem" is assessed, that entity, by definition, contains no strengths or positive processes which can be used for change and enhancement. Problems are problems. . . . As the definition[of synergy] implies, strength is available to the process if the individuals are not of one mind with respect to point of view. There is creative energy to be tapped within the tensions created by appositional frames of reference. Thus, from the liaison psychologist's point of view, perspectives which might be deemed harmful or maladaptive by others are seen as a necessary and useful part of the change process. (Plas, 1981, p. 75)

A win/win philosophy is a natural companion to the idea of synergic power. Within this model, the liaison specialist enters the situation with a view toward facilitating the creation of a solution that finds no one gaining at the expense of another's loss.

Rather than attempting to "fix kids," the liaison specialist strives toward creating relationships that are more responsive to the needs of the total ecology. The liaison specialist in the schools follows a seven-stage process*:

1. entering the system
2. mapping the ecology
3. assessing the ecology
4. creating the vision of change
5. coordinating and communicating
6. reassessing
7. evaluating

While the procedures associated with each step have been described elsewhere, it will be helpful to comment here on stage 4, creating the vision of change. Central to the effective use of this stage of intervention development is a major meeting of all the salient persons from the child's most influential systems. The liaison specialist acts in a managerial role at this meeting, directing energy toward the creation of a vision for how things might be different—not only for the child but for all concerned. Natural differences of opinion are respected and encouraged; natural strengths in the system and individuals also are highlighted. The focus here is on the "vision." Without hopes and ideas about how things can be better, systems, as well as individuals, are often immobilized.

As is the case with a variety of other systems approaches to mental health in the schools, a face-to-face meeting of the principal parties to the situation is absolutely necessary in order for the effectiveness of the school-based liaison method to be realized. In contrast to other approaches, the liaison approach in the schools relies heavily on natural discord and intervention per se begins with creation of a vision rather than creation of behavioral plans. Behavior change is expected to emerge from other stages of the process.

APPROACHES IN THE FIELD OF SCHOOL PSYCHOLOGY

Hannafin and Witt (1983) have devised a method for intervention by the school psychologist at the level of the school system. They note the challenges school psychologists have faced over the years as they have attempted to define their role while beset by pressures from administrators, teachers, parents, the profession, and various government mandates. They call for broadening the role of the school psychologist to include system intervention functions as well as direct service. Their approach (Hannafin & Witt,

---

*Cf., McDonald, n.d., for a complementary discussion of the stages of the liaison function.

1983, pp. 131–134) concentrates on effective system level analysis, defining five typical problem areas:

1. ineffective interaction among components
2. missing system components
3. inadequate articulation of system structure and contingencies
4. inadequate management or implementation of system operation
5. poor system organization

Hannafin and Witt discuss each of these in terms of possible responses by the school psychologist.

Maher (1981) has produced an approach at the interface of behavioral and systems psychology. His work emphasizes the production of systems-related behavioral outcome goals subsequent to an intensive systems assessment phase. Like Hannafin and Witt, Maher believes that the school psychologist's most effective role may eventually lie in systems-oriented interventions.

Curtis and Yager (1981) apply systems thinking to the supervision of school psychologists. Their approach concentrates on development of a collaborative effort between psychologist and supervisor. Attention is given to the permeability of system boundaries outside the schools, which the school psychologist is expected to cross. Thus, in addition to evaluation of intraperson variables, the supervisor becomes concerned with the psychologist's interactions within and across systems that are important to the welfare of children.

CLASSROOM ENVIRONMENT APPROACHES

In recent years, Trickett and his colleagues (Billington, Washington, & Trickett, 1981; Ellison & Trickett, 1978; Trickett, 1978; Trickett, McConahay, Phillips, & Ginter, in press; Trickett & Quinlan, 1979; Trickett & Wilkinson, 1979) extended the original work of Moos and Trickett (1974) on the Classroom Environment Scale (CES) to a variety of intervention methods. These are systems-oriented approaches inspired by the social environment work of Roger Barker (see Chapter 4). The CES is an instrument for measuring the perceived environment of a classroom. Relying on the averaged perceptions of members of the environment, the CES is composed of dimensions that tap various aspects of classroom life, such as Order and Organization, Student Affiliation, Rule Emphasis, and Competition. Trickett and his colleagues conducted factor analysis of the instrument and used it in a variety of settings for intervention as well as assessment. The Trickett approach is more measurement oriented than any of the others considered in this book. The original theory behind his work was based on the rationale that pooled perceptions of an environment could represent a useful reflection of that environment (cf., Moos, 1974).

This work deserves attention within a discussion of systems approaches to psychology in the schools because the emphasis here primarily is on the social environment created by group culture (and, secondarily, its relationship to the physical environment). Rather than focusing on individuals within the schools, the classroom environment approach identifies the most central school-based behavior setting (in the Barker sense) — the classroom — and focuses diagnostic and intervention attention upon it. Trickett and Wilkinson (1979) have noted that one's understanding of a classroom environment is influenced greatly by the decision to analyze it in terms of individual or averaged group perceptions. They have written that the

> importance of the distinction is both conceptual and methodological. Conceptually, if one analyzes perceived environment data using individuals as the unit, one finds, strictly speaking, individual differences in how environments are perceived, not differences in environments per se. Methodologically, if the intent is to describe environments rather than individuals, statistical analyses should be based on group, not individual, data. (p. 498)

Trickett and his associates operate from a different frame of reference than family system therapists or others who design systems methodologies for use in the schools. In other models, an understanding of the group is captured by observing the communication patterns among members of the system. What passes between and among people is of primary importance. These methods emphasize observation of the here and now and rarely employ any normative testing. In contrast, Trickett and his colleagues use retrospective information provided by people in schools, who respond to a paper-and-pencil test associated with useful normative procedures for interpreting results. Among other topics, this work has focused on high schools, junior high schools, principals, and traditional and alternative schools. The work is carefully done and is embedded within a provocative theoretical rationale. Thus, those who wish to attach a research component to their intervention efforts, or who wish to begin systems work by producing an initial understanding of the social climates of the target schools and classrooms, are urged to consult this important work.

A RELATED SYSTEMIC APPROACH

Fine and Holt (1983) produced a family systems perspective toward work with school-based problems. Of the approaches available in the school psychological literature today, this one is most closely akin to the spirit of the systemic work represented so heavily in this book. Coming out of the school psychology tradition, Fine and Holt consulted the family therapy literature, read some of the Milan Associates work, and outlined an intervention approach that is consonant with their synthesis of systemic theory and other versions of family therapy (e.g., Bowen, 1978; Minuchin & Fishman, 1981; Watzlawick, Weakland, & Fisch, 1974). Because their thinking is influenced by family theorists who work within traditions other than the systemic, their version of practice is aptly labeled a *systems approach* rather than a *systemic approach*.

Theoretically, Fine and Holt rely on the distinction they draw between systemic and linear thinking. With the exception of their construal of causal relationships, their presentation is quite complementary to some of what has been said earlier within that frame of reference. They note that we have typically engaged in "straight line" thinking as we attempt to understand the problems of children in schools. They further point out that a systemic viewpoint implies a circular, rather than linear, process of causality. However, their interpretation of this fundamental idea represents a mix of several systems orientations rather than major indebtedness to Selvini-Palazzoli and her associates. They write, for example, that, "each 'cause' of behavior is really an effect of a prior cause, and each effect causes a later event" (Fine & Holt, 1983, pp. 59–60).

In addition to their desire to adopt a nonlinear perspective, their intervention method conveys a recognition of the communication rules that guide systems and the limitations of contemporary language. Fine and Holt (1983, p. 61) believe that

> The goals of a systemic approach would be to assist the respective systems (home and school) to emotionally disengage themselves so that they can collaborate helpfully on behalf of the child, to "normalize" the child's position in each system, and subsequently to help the child effect a more appropriate school adjustment.

Thus, unlike the approach developed in this book, and in a fashion similar to others who have designed systems psychology processes for the schools, their approach works at the interface of the home and school. An initial interview with parents, teachers, and the child produces information concerning power relationships, system rigidity, enmeshment of family members, and mechanisms for family maintenance. These writers advocate the use of some forms of circular questioning, such as "having people describe how they think other persons would define the situation or problem" (Fine & Holt, 1983, p. 62). "Taking sides" and offering paradoxes are also seen as useful.

While the Fine and Holt approach is not elaborated in great detail, it, nonetheless, is well within the growing systemic tradition. As they think about issues related to the practice of this type of intervention in the schools, they find a need to offer a set of cautions. For example:

> Training, practice, supervision, and feedback are extremely important if consultants are to utilize effectively a systems orientation. School-based consultants

should approach cautiously the extensive use of systemic intervention without proper training and a period of supervised practice. . . .

The techniques that the consultant might use of a paradoxical or reframing nature, or the use of specific directives, cast the relationship with the teacher in a different light. This is potentially a professional ethics issue in terms of the indirectness of manipulativeness of the relationship, and needs to be thought through by each practitioner. (Fine & Holt, 1983, pp. 64-65)

Fine and Holt offer an interesting approach, which incorporates aspects of several important current family systems orientations. However, they acknowledge greatest indebtedness to systemic ways of devising intervention strategies.

11

THE PAST AND THE FUTURE

It is intelligent to ask two questions: (1) Is it possible? (2) Can I do it? But it is unintelligent to ask these questions: (1) Is it real? (2) Has my neighbor Christopherson done it?

— Søren Kierkegaard

Groups have been around for a long, long time. Despite that, few major thinkers, outside the realms of politics and sociology, have attempted to understand their influence on the life of the individual. Thus, if one wants to think deeply about the group in Western society, especially in America, one must turn to political theorists, sociologists, and a few philosophers. In psychology, interest in understanding systems has developed largely within social psychology, where the emphasis has been on research. Traditionally, psychology has been more interested in collecting data about group functioning than in trying to change it.

Why has applied psychology's interest in understanding human systems been so late in coming? Why have natural groups been considered seriously as a target for intervention only during the past 15 years or so?

About 25 years ago, the group dynamics movement, originated by Kurt Lewin, picked up speed. A proliferation of group-oriented intervention methods exploded onto the scene in the late 1960s. Most of these were developed for use with artificial or temporary groups, which came together for an evening or a weekend. Uniformly, their purposes centered on individual growth and development. The welfare of the group was not so much at stake as was the welfare of the individual participant. A notable exception to this trend were the efforts by the National Training Laboratory, which incorporated somewhat similar techniques but was more involved in working with such natural groups as those found in business or industry. Still, however, the development of the individual was a primary goal of the process.

In a few isolated places, such as the Palo Alto veterans organization, therapists worked with intact natural groups, such as families. However, this work was not seized upon quickly by the typical psychologist. Individual therapy remained the modus operandi for practicing clinicians. It had worked for Sigmund Freud and Carl Rogers, and it was likely that those initial efforts could only be improved upon.

The early pioneers in family therapy began working only a few short years ago. Hoffman (1981) has begun to identify a "second generation" of family therapists, but it is a bit of a stretch to think in terms of a second generation when those cited as members of the first generation are still so alive and changing. Clearly, intervening with natural groups, such as families and classrooms, is a recent phenomenon within applied psychology. Prior to the family movement, groupwork in natural settings was still oriented, in large measure, toward the individual.

There are at least two major reasons why intervention with natural groups has been slow to develop in this country. The first relates to the somewhat peculiar American emphasis on individualism. The functionalist psychology that developed here during the first quarter of this century was almost religiously devoted to the individual. The testing movement was born here, for example, and remains a national psychological preoccupation to this day. We want to understand individual differences. We, as a culture, believe that those differences, stirred around in a melting pot, have made us the nation we are—and of which we are proud. In psychology's past, an exploration of groups was considered a European adventure. The European mind could appreciate a concept like the "zeitgeist," an American mind could only get to an understanding of an idea like the "standard deviation." Many Americans had suffered in other countries at the hands of the "group." This country was to be the place that honored the rights of the individual.

A second concern that prevented easy concentration on the group rather than the individual grew out of the American fixation on individualism. This is the equally peculiar American tendency to be unable even to *see* the group when individuals are present. That is, it remains difficult for us to observe a group without drifting toward a focus on an individual or two within that group. As the Gestalt psychologists pointed out around 1913, this phenomenon is partially a characteristic that all human beings share. We need to develop a figure from a ground in order to have something meaningful on which to concentrate. Theoretically, however, it is conceivable that the group becomes figure set against any other natural perceptual ground. It is just plain hard for Americans to do that, however. We are much too fascinated with the individual's looks, personality, values, attitudes, and so forth. The best we can pull off is an occasional glance at averaged looks, personalities, values, attitudes, and so forth.

Whether the tendency to regard individuals rather than groups is shared equally by all human beings or whether it is exaggerated within American culture, it creates methodological difficulties when a desire to understand the group predominates. It is difficult to know just where to *look* to see a group. Surely, it is true that we cannot hold two thoughts in our heads at one time or a collection of individuals in our field of vision. Given that reality, there really may be no group to observe. Maybe there are only individuals who call themselves members of this group or that.

In American psychology, we have generally responded to this dilemma by producing averages and normative information based on those averages. We try to describe the American family by noting that it has 2.3 children; and the polls seem to represent as good a way as any of letting us know which politicians, television shows, and products our families favor. The Moos and Trickett work cited in the previous chapter provides excellent rationale for the strategy of considering pooled perceptions as representative of the phenomenon of interest.

Bateson and others in this country who originated and graced the family therapy movement (e.g. Haley, 1964 ; Watzlawick, Jackson, & Bearin, 1967) began to suspect that another way of understanding the family as group was possible and necessary. However, inspired by this work, and using some importantly different perspectives, it was a team of Italian therapists who gave us systemic theory and methodology.

While it is not astonishing that systemic thinking was originally a European import, it also is not surprising that when ways of truly beginning to understand groups became available, we began to call these groups *systems*. The idea of group implies a collection of individuals. A system implies an organized set of relations composing a whole. What some family therapists from all continents have deduced (and induced) is that observing a family requires intentional abandonment of the individuals composing it. The process requires observation of patterns and rhythms and redundancies. Ultimately, it is not important that a theme in process of development moves from a particular person to another particular person. Within this frame of reference, it matters that themes develop by rolling from one location in the system to others in recurrent, almost predictable patterns. In some families, themes seem to be created at a central point and radiated outward; in others, the ball rolls from one portion of the court to the others before an identifiable theme has emerged.

Thus, a fundamental issue associated with the life and growth of applied systems thinking in general, and systemic work in particular, is whether the ability to continue focusing attention on the system can be maintained. Is this an idea whose time has come or an idea that has come too quickly? I am reminded at this point of some of the early work in behaviorism, which found those empiricists concerned about the concept of "instinctual drift," a tendency for difficult learned behaviors in certain animal species to weaken across time. Some speculated that, eventually, behaviors would *necessarily* drift toward the instinctual rather than learned response. It is possible that an analogous tendency might occur with the phenomenon of systemic thinking. If this perspective is culturally too difficult to maintain, there may be a return to more individualized ways of approaching human problems. Like most things, the eventual outcome probably will be at least partially dependent upon the successes we experience with the model. If systems approaches provide us with effective ways of attacking old problems, we are likely to develop them even further.

SYSTEMIC FUTURES IN THE SCHOOLS

One of the major criticisms of systemic family therapy has been that the cost is prohibitive for most. The majority of systemic techniques employ four professional persons for anywhere from 2 to 5 hours per session. Thus, the cost to the family or third party payer is very large. Some teams have maneuvered around this by using free doctoral student help, reducing the number of therapists, or providing this kind of service to a very limited number of families through a public-supported agency. Those who are persuaded by the systemic approach note that even though each session is expensive, far fewer sessions are required, and individual therapy for each family member would result in the same expenditure of money. Despite these rationales, the issue of expense has not been adequately resolved within the profession.

The situation within the public schools is remarkably different than that in family work. The application of good systemic work can be cost-effective within the schools. A team of four persons can work with as many as 25 persons within a given focus-group. The sessions may last from 2 to 5 hours across 8 months or so. On the average, then, 32 hours of actual intervention time may be expended on 25 persons by four professional staff members. Such a ratio is usual, customary, and reasonable within the school. In addition, no money crosses hands. Through public mandate, psychological support services are supported by tax funds. Thus, what may well prove to be the biggest stumbling block within the private mental health field is not a significant problem within the public schools.

The required preparation time will likely be a major difficulty in the schools. Finding the time to recruit team members and engaging in 8–10 months of concentrated team education will prove problematic in most cases. It is likely that the time will be taken from personal rather than professional lives. It also is likely that the kind of commitment required by such a process will ensure the involvement of those sufficiently sensitive and dedicated to become excellent systemic interventionists. Those who attempt these processes without adequate preparation will likely fail.

Another concern for those who wish to engage in this work in the schools is that there, the team will be relating to a system within a system (within a system). This creates an additional set of contingencies (see Chapter 7), which must be acknowledged and adequately responded to if things are to go well. However, these contingencies need not be a burden; they represent challenges that undoubtedly can result in much team and individual satisfaction.

Closely allied to this notion is the necessity for considering parental and public rights within the schools. Chief among these has been the right to information. Potentially delicate situations can exist when parents (or school board members) indicate a desire to know the specifics of "what is going on" within a systemic focus-group. I recommend that the routine ways such things are handled within a school system be adopted in these cases as well. If a school psychologist were to engage in a classroom-oriented intervention that was not systems-oriented, how would the parents be informed about the specifics? No matter what strategies are chosen, it is important that all parties principal to the intervention contribute to the decision to operate in that particular way. In all cases, agreements on the front end will reduce misunderstandings and hassles later on.

FUTURE NEEDS

One of the major contributions systemic school psychology might make is to the research literature. Currently, there is a lamentable lack of research that focuses on an understanding of systemic processes. There are many case studies and clinical reports but little to no empirical work is available. Therefore, I recommend that those who engage in this work in the schools contract with the school system's evaluation specialist or, perhaps, with the team's outside consultant or with another outside source to devise research methodology for one or more of the interventions conducted in a given setting. Offering the results of such studies to the literature would create an invaluable source of empirical information concerning systemic intervention.

In addition to producing good research, additional strategies applicable to schools are needed. Storytelling is a good example of a heretofore less often used method that has much applicability in the schools. As more people engage in this kind of professional practice, other useful strategies will undoubtedly develop.

FINAL THOUGHTS

Systemic psychology is an interesting and promising new approach to working with human problems. Its applicability to the schools should be thoroughly tested; its promise should be developed in these settings. Systemic strategies are unusual strategies. They call for attention to communication rules rather than to individuals; they require that the practitioner abandon important notions of causality in favor of observing patterns through analogical reasoning. Somewhere in the midst of all that is new to think about in systemic psychology is the issue of professional ethics. When systemic work (or any other work, for that matter) devolves into manipulation or "game playing" in the cruelest sense of that term, it is time to quit — or to at least take stock of its goals. When professionals play respectfully, when they enjoy the challenges of putting together pieces of a puzzle and the stimulation brought to the task by delightful and ingenious family and focus-group members, the situation contains little danger of ethical violations. A sense of humor and a genuine enjoyment of people is probably a prerequisite for this kind of work, as it is for effective work within any psychological persuasion. A genuine caring about people also helps assist us through the rough spots.

Such a courteous stance is probably even more important for school-based intervention than for private work. A multiplicity of problems and demands face those who work each day in the complex system known as the public schools. Sometimes, in that setting, only a desire to care and to be respectful is possible on any given day. We can get hold of the desire but not the behaviors. That's O.K., I think. Sometimes that will get us through, too.

REFERENCES

Ames, Adelbert, Jr. (1960). *The morning notes of Adelbert Ames, Jr.* New Brunswick, NJ: Rutgers University Press.
Aponte, H. J. (1976). The family-school interview: An eco-structural approach. *Family Process, 15,* 303-311.
Barker, R. G. (1968). *Ecological psychology.* Palo Alto, CA: Stanford University Press.
Barker, R. G., & Associates. (1978). *Habitats, environments, and human behavior.* San Francisco: Jossey-Bass.
Barker, R. G., & Wright, H. F. (1955). *Midwest and its children.* New York: Harper & Row. Reprinted by Archon Books, Hamden, CT, 1971.
Bateson, G. (1972). *Steps to an ecology of mind.* New York: Ballantine.
Bateson, G. (1979). *Mind and nature: A necessary unity.* New York: E. P. Dutton.
Bateson, G., Jackson, D. D., Haley, J., & Weakland, J. (1956). Toward a theory of schizophrenia. *Behavioral Science, 1,* 251-264.
Berger, P. L., & Luckmann, T. (1967). *The social construction of reality.* Garden City, NY: Doubleday Anchor Books.
Billington, R. J., Washington, L. A., & Trickett, E. J. (1981). The research relationship in community research: An inside view from public school principals. *American Journal of Community Psychology, 9*(4), 461-479.
Bowen, M. (1960). A family concept of schizophrenia. In D. D. Jackson (Ed.), *The etiology of schizophrenia.* New York: Basic Books. Reprinted in Bowen, M., *Family therapy in clinical practice.* New York: Jason Aronson, 1978.
Bowen, Murray. (1978). *Family Therapy in Clinical Practice.* New York: Jason Aronson.
Cantril, H., Ames, A., Jr., Hastorf, A. H., & Ittelson, W. H. (1949a). Psychology and scientific research. I. The nature of scientific inquiry. *Science, 110,* 461-464.
Cantril, H., Ames, A., Jr., Hastorf, A. H., & Ittelson, W. H. (1949b). Psychology and scientific research. II. Scientific theory and scientific method. *Science, 110,* 491-496.
Cantril, H., Ames, A., Jr., Hastorf, A. H., & Ittelson, W. H. (1949c). Psychology and scientific research. III. The transactional view in psychological research. *Science, 110,* 517-522.
Capra, R. (1975). *The Tao of physics.* Berkeley: Shambhala.
Capra, F. (1982). *The turning point: Science, society, and the rising culture.* New York: Simon & Schuster.

REFERENCES

Chavis, D. M., Hogge, J. H., McMillan, D. W., & Wandersman, A. (1986). Sense of Community through Brunswik's lens: A first look. *Journal of Community Psychology, 14*(1), 24-40.

Craig, J. H., & Craig, M. (1974). *Synergic power: Beyond domination and permissiveness.* California: Proactive Press.

Curtis, M. J., & Yager, G. G. (1981). A systems model for the supervision of school psychological services. *School Psychology Review, 10*(4), 425-433.

Dell, P. F. (1981). Some irreverent thoughts on paradox. *Family Process, 20,* 37-51.

Dell, P. F. (1982). Beyond homeostasis. *Family Process, 21,* 57-64.

Dewey, J., & Bentley, A. (1949). Knowing and the known. Republished in R. Handy & E. C. Harwood (Eds.), *Useful procedures of inquiry.* Great Barrington, MA: Behavior Research Council, 1973.

Dokecki, P. R. (1977). The liaison perspective on the enhancement of human development: Theoretical, historical, and experiential background. *Journal of Community Psychology, 5,* 13-17.

Dokecki, P. R. (1978). A transactional perspective on the interrelationship of the societal power structure, the mental health establishment, the individual, and the community: A commentary on Nassi. *Journal of Community Psychology, 6,* 19-21.

Dokecki, P. R. (1983). The place of values in the world of psychology and public policy. *The Peabody Journal of Education: The Legacy of Nicholas Hobbs, 60*(3), 108-125.

Ellison, T. A., & Trickett, E. J. (1978). Environmental structure and the perceived similarity–satisfaction relationship: Traditional and alternative schools. *Journal of Personality, 46,* 57-71.

Emery, S. (1978). *Actualizations: You don't have to rehearse to be yourself.* Garden City, NY: Doubleday.

Engel, G. L. (1977, April 8). The need for a new medical model: A challenge for biomedicine. *Science.*

Fine, M. J., & Holt, P. (1983). Intervening with school problems: A family systems perspective. *Psychology in the Schools, 20,* 59-66.

Gibbs, J. C. (1979). The meaning of ecologically oriented inquiry in contemporary psychology. *American Psychologist, 34* (2), 127-140.

Glidewell, J. C. (1972). Helping systems. In S. E. Golann & C. Eisdorfer (Eds.), *Handbook of community mental health,* pp. 230-246. New York: Appleton-Century-Crofts.

Gray, S. W. (1963). *The psychologist in the schools.* New York: Holt, Rinehart & Winston.

Guillemin, V. (1968). *The story of quantum mechanics.* New York: Charles Scribner's Sons.

Haley, J. (1963). *Strategies of psychotherapy.* New York: Grune & Stratton.

Haley, J. (1973). *Uncommon therapy.* New York: Ballantine Books.

Hannafin, M. J., & Witt, J. C. (1983). System intervention and the school psychologist: Maximizing interplay among roles and functions. *Professional Psychology: Research and Practice, 14*(1), 128-136.

Hastorf, A. H., & Cantril, H. (1954). They saw a game. *Journal of Abnormal and Social Psychology, 49,* 129-134.

Heisenberg, W. (1959). *Physics and philosophy.* New York: Harper.

Hilgard, E. R. (Ed.). (1978). *American psychology in historical perspective: Addresses of the presidents of the American Psychological Association.* Washington, DC: American Psychological Association.

Hobbs, N. (1966). Helping disturbed children: Psychological and ecological strategies. *American Psychologist, 21,* 1105–1115.
Hobbs, N. (1975). *The futures of children: Categories, labels, and their consequences.* San Francisco: Jossey-Bass.
Hobbs, N., et al. (1979). *Exceptional teaching for exceptional learning.* New York: Ford Foundation.
Hobbs, N., Dokecki, P. R., Hoover-Dempsey, K. V., Moroney, R. N., Shayne, M. W., & Weeks, K. H. (1984). *Strengthening families.* San Francisco: Jossey-Bass.
Hoffman, L. (1981). *Foundations of family therapy: A conceptual framework for systems change.* New York: Basic Books.
Hofstadter, D. R. (1980). *Godel, Escher, Bach: An eternal golden braid.* New York: Vintage Books.
Keeney, B. P. (1983). *Aesthetics of change.* New York: The Guilford Press.
Kelly, J. G. (1968). Toward an ecological conception of preventive interventions. In J. Carter, Jr. (Ed.), *Research contributions from psychology to community mental health,* pp. 75–99. New York: Behavioral Publications.
Kuhn, T. S. (1962). *The structure of scientific revolutions.* Chicago: The University of Chicago Press.
Langer, S. K. (1942). *Philosophy in a new key.* Cambridge, MA: Harvard University Press.
Langer, S. K. (1962). *Philosophical sketches.* Baltimore, MD: The Johns Hopkins Press.
Lee, D. (1950). Codifications of reality. Lineal and nonlineal. *Psychosomatic Medicine, 12*(2), 89–97. Reprinted in Ornstein, R. E. (Ed.), The nature of human consciousness, pp. 128–142. San Francisco: W. H. Freeman & Co., 1973.
Lenzer, G. (Ed.). (1975). *Auguste Comte and positivism: The essential writings.* Chicago: University of Chicago Press.
Lewin, K. (1951). *Field theory in social science.* New York: Harper & Row.
Lightfoot, S. L. (1978). *World apart.* New York: Basic Books.
Lightfoot, S. L. (1983). *The good high school.* New York: Basic Books.
Lincoln, Y. S., & Guba, E. G. (1985). *Naturalistic inquiry.* Beverly Hills, CA: Sage Publications.
London, P. (1964). *The modes and morals of psychotherapy.* New York: Holt, Rinehart, & Winston.
Lusterman, D. D. (1985). An ecosystemic approach to family-school problems. *The American Journal of Family Therapy, 13*(1), 22–30.
Maher, C. A. (1981). Intervention with school social systems: A behavioral–systems approach. *School Psychology Review, 10*(4), 499–508.
Marrow, A. J. (1969). *The practical theorist: The life and work of Kurt Lewin.* New York: Basic Books.
Maturana, H. (1975). The organization of the living: A theory of the living organization. *International Journal of Man-Machine Studies, 7,* 313–332.
Maturana, H., & Varela, F. J. (1980). *Autopoiesis and cognition: The realization of the living.* Dordrecht, Netherlands: D. Reidel Publishing Co. McDonald, C. (n.d.). *The liaison teacher-counselor in a re-educational school.* Final Report: NIMH Grant No. MH14645.
McDonald, C. (n.d.) *The liaison teacher-counselor in a re-educational school.* NIMH Grant No. MH 14645. State of Tennessee Re-Ed program. Nashville, TN.
McMillan, D. W., & Chavis, D. M. (1986). Sense of community: A definition and theory. *Journal of Community Psychology, 14*(1), 6–23.

REFERENCES

Minuchin, C., & Fishman, H. (1981). *Family therapy techniques.* Cambridge, MA: Harvard University Press.

Moos, R. H. (1974). *Evaluating treatment environments: A social ecological approach.* New York: Wiley.

Moos, R. H., & Trickett, E. J. (1974). *Classroom environment scale manual.* Palo Alto, CA: Consulting Psychologists Press.

Moynihan, J. (Ed.). *Who is the client?* Washington, DC: American Psychological Association.

Murrell, S. A. (1973). *Community psychology and social systems.* New York: Behavioral Publications.

Myrdal, G. (1969). *Objectivity in social research.* New York: Pantheon.

Newbrough, J. R. (1977a). Liaison services in the community context. *Journal of Community Psychology, 5,* 24–27.

Newbrough, J. R. (1977b). Preliminary plans for the implementation of conference recommendations. In I. Iscoe, B. S. Bloom, & I. C. Spielberger (Eds.), *Community psychology in transition.* Washington, DC: Hemisphere Publishing Corporation.

Newbrough, J. R. (1984). Editorial: 1984 — Prospects for the field of community psychology. *Journal of Community Psychology, 12,* 91–98.

Newbrough, J. R., & Chavis, D. M. (Eds.). (1986a). Psychological sense of community. I. Theory and concepts. *Journal of Community Psychology, 14*(1), Special issue.

Newbrough, J. R., & Chavis, D. M. (Eds.). (1986b). Psychological sense of community. II. Research and application. *Journal of Community Psychology, 14*(2), Special issue.

Oppenheimer, J. R. (1956). Analogy in science. *American Psychologist, 11,* 127–135.

Page, P. (1983). *The process of change.* New York: The Guilford Press.

Papp, P. (1983). *The process of change.* Guilford Family Therapy Series. New York: Guilford Press.

Penn, P. (1982). Circular questioning. *Family Process, 21,* 267–280.

Plas, J. M. (1981). The psychologist in the school community: A liaison role. *School Psychology Review, 10,* 72–81.

Plas, J. M. (1985). Sudden change: Family therapy and community psychology possibilities. *Journal of Community Psychology, 13* (3), 311–317.

Plas, J. M., & Dokecki, P. R. (1982). Philosophy-based education: A transactional approach. *Professional Psychology, 12* (2).

Plas, J. M., Hoover-Dempsey, K. V., & Wallston, B. S. (1985). A conceptualization of professional women's interpersonal fields: Social support, reference group, and persons-to-be-reckoned-with. In I. G. Sarason & B. R. Sarason (Eds.), *Social support; Theory, research and applications* (NATO ASI Series). Dordrecht/Boston: Martinus Nijhoff Publishers.

Platt, J. (1970). Hierarchical growth. *Bulletin of Atomic Scientists, 26*(9), 2–4, 46–48.

Prigogine, I. (1980). *From being to becoming: Time and complexity in the physical sciences.* San Francisco: W. H. Freeman & Co.

Ratner, S. & Altman, J. (Eds.) (1964). *John Dewey and Arthur F. Bentley: A philosophical correspondence, 1932–1951.* New Brunswick, N.J.: Rutgers University Press.

Raeburn, J. (1986). Towards a sense of community: comprehensive community projects and community houses. *Journal of Community Psychology, 14*(4).

Ratner, S., & Altman, J. (Eds.). (1964). *John Dewey and Arthur F. Bentley: A Phil-*

osophical Correspondence, 1932-1951. New Brunswick, NJ: Rutgers University Press.
Ricoeur, P. (1978). The problem of the foundation of moral philosophy. *Philosophy Today, 22,* 175-192.
Riceour, P. (1983). Informal discussion at Peabody College of Vanderbilt University, Nashville, TN.
Rusell, B. (1960). *Our knowledge of the external world.* New York: Mentor Books.
Sarason, S. (1974). *The psychological sense of community: Prospects for a community psychology.* San Francisco: Jossey-Bass.
Sarason, S. (1981). *Psychology misdirected.* New York: The Free Press.
Sarason, S. (1986). The emergence of a conceptual center. *Journal of Community Psychology, 14*(4).
Selvini-Palazzoli, M. (1974). *Self-starvation.* London: Chaucer Publishing.
Selvini-Palazzoli, M., Boscolo, L., Cecchin, G., & Prata, G. (1980). Hypothesizing—circularity—neutrality: Three guidelines for the conductor of the session. *Family Process, 19,* 3-12.
Selvini-Palazzoli, M., Cecchin, G., Prata, G., & Boscolo, L. (1978). *Paradox and counterparadox: A new model in the therapy of the family in schizophrenic transaction.* New York: Jason Aronson.
Shands, H. C. (1971). *The war with words.* The Hague, Netherlands: Mouton.
Shrady, M. (1972). *Moments of insight.* New York: Harper Colophon Books.
Spencer-Brown, L. (1973). *Laws of form.* New York: Bantam.
Strupp, H. (1984). *Psychology in a new key.* New York: Basic Books.
Stucky, P., & Newbrough, J. R. (1983). Mentally retarded persons in the community. In K. T. Kernon, M. J. Begab, & R. B. Edgerton (Eds.), *Environments and behavior: The adaptation of mentally retarded persons,* pp. 19-29. Baltimore: University Park Press.
The Larry P. Decision. (1980). *School Psychology Review, 9,* (2).
The Future of Psychology in the Schools: Proceedings of the Spring Hill Symposium. (1981). *School Psychology Review, 10*(2), special joint issue: American Psychological Association and National Association of School Psychologists.
Tittler, B. I., & Cook, V. J. (1981). Relationships among family, school, and clinic: Toward a systems approach. *Journal of Clinical Child Psychology,* Fall, 184-187.
Torrance, E. P. (1961). Factors affecting creative thinking in children: An interim research report. *Merrill-Palmer Quarterly, 7,* 171-180.
Trickett, E. J. (1978). Towards a social ecological conception of adolescent development: Normative data on contrasting types of public school classrooms. *Child Development, 49,* 408-414.
Trickett, E. J., & Quinlan, D. M. (1979). Three domains of classroom environment: Factor analysis of the classroom environment scale. *American Journal of Community Psychology, 7,* 279-291.
Trickett, E. J., & Wilkinson, L. (1979). Using individual or group scores on perceived environment scales: Classroom environment scale as example. *American Journal of Community Psychology, 7,* 497-502.
Trickett, E. J., McConahay, J. B., Phillips, D., & Ginter, M. A, (in press). Natural experiments and the educational context: The environment and effects of an alternative inner city public school on adolescents. *American Journal of Community Psychology.*
von Foerster, H. (1973). Cybernetics of cybernetics (physiology of revolution). *The Cybernitician, 1,* 31-43.

REFERENCES

von Foerster, H. (1976). Author of various chapters in K. Wilson (Ed.), *The collected works of the Biological Computer Laboratory*. Peoria: Illinois Blueprint Corp.

Vygotsky, L. S. (1962). *Thought and language*. Cambridge, MA: M.I.T. Press.

Watzlawick, P., Jackson, D., & Beavin, J. (1967). *Pragmatics of Human Communication*. New York: W. W. Norton.

Watzlawick, P., Weakland, J., & Fisch, R. (1974). *Change*. New York: Norton.

Whorf, B. L. (1941). The relation of habitual thought and behavior to language. In L. Spier (Ed.), *Language, culture, and personality*. Menasha, WI: Sapir Memorial Publication Fund.

Williams, J. S. (1977). Liaison services as reflected in a case study. *Journal of Community Psychology, 5,* 18–23.

Zukav, G. (1979). *The dancing Wu-Li masters: An overview of the new physics*. New York: William Morrow & Co.

AUTHOR INDEX

Altman, J., 21
Ames, A., 19–20
Aponte, H. J., 137–138
Aristotle, 4

Barker, R., 26–29
Bateson, G., xiv, xvi, 10–13, 33, 41, 43–44, 50, 60, 61–64, 70, 77, 79–80, 82, 147
Bateson, M. C., 10
Beavin, J., 147
Bentley, A. F., xiii, xvi, 17, 21–22, 50, 52, 59–60
Berger, P. L., 14, 50
Billington, R. J., 141
Bloch, D., 48
Bohm, D., 14
Bohr, N., 14
Boscolo, L., 33–34
Bowen, M., 34

Cantril, H., 19–21
Capra, F., xvi, 5, 13–16, 31, 43, 54, 67
Cecchin, G., 33–34
Chavis, D., 28–29
Comte, A., 77–78
Confucius, 4
Conlan, J., 55
Cook, V. J., 138
Craig, J. H., 139r
Craig, M., 139
Curtis, M. J., 141

Dell, P. F., 41
Dewey, J., xiii, xvi, 17, 21–22, 50, 52, 54, 59–60, 85–87
Dokecki, P. R., xiii, 22, 29–30, 31–32, 139

Ellison, T. A, 141
Emery, S., 81
Engel, G. L., 15

Fine, M. J., 142–144
Fisch, R., 143
Fishman, H., 143

Ginter, M. A., 141
Glidewell, J. C., 30
Guba, E. G., 55, 81
Guillemin, V., 14

Haley, J., 10, 147
Hannafin, M. J., 140–141
Hastorf, A., 19
Heisenberg, 14
Hobbs, N., 138–140
Hobbes, T., 5, 31–32
Hoffman, L., xvi, 33, 40–43, 60, 146a
Hofstadter, D. R., 62
Holt, P., 142–144
Hoover-Dempsey, K., 24
Hume, D., 5, 55

Ittelson, W. H., 19

AUTHOR INDEX

Jackson, D., 10, 147
Jeans, J., 67
Jung, C., 63

Kant, I., 55
Keeney, B. P., xvi, 33, 43-46, 61
Kelly, J., 26
Kohler, W., 18-19
Kuhn, T., 5

Langer, S. K., 14, 50
Lao Tsu, 4
Lee, D., 58
Lewin, K., xiii, 24, 145
Lightfoot, S. L., 102-103
Lincoln, Y. S., 55, 81
Locke, J., 5
London, P., 31
Luckman, T., 14, 50
Lusterman, D. D., 136-138

Maher, C. A., 141
Malinowski, B., 58
Maturana, H., xiv, xvi, 16-17, 41, 43
McConahay, J. B., 141
McDonald, C., 140
Milan Associates, 33-42, 46-48, 50, 60-61, 73-74, 82, 143
Minuchin, C., 143
Moos, R. H., 141
Mounihan, J., 99
Myrdal, G., 31
Murrell, S., 25

Newbrough, J. R., 26, 28-30, 139

Oppenheimer, R., 6

Papp, P., xvi, 33, 46-48
Phillips, D., 141
Piaget, J., 86-88

Plas, J. M., xiii, 22, 24, 40-41, 77-78, 139-140
Plato, 4
Platt, J., 41, 78
Prata, G., 33-34
Prigogine, I., 16, 41, 77

Quinlan, D. M., 141

Raeburn, J., 29
Ratner, S., 21
Ricoeur, P., 31, 80-81
Russell, B., 15, 64

Sarason, S., 28
Selvini-Palazzoli, M., xiv, 33-40, 48
Shands, H., 14, 52, 60
Socrates, 4
Spencer-Brown, L., 44
Stucky, P., 29-30

Tittler, B. I., 138
Tricket, E. J., 141-142

Varella, F. J., 16, 43
von Foerster, H., 43

Vygotsky, L. S., 52

Wallston, B. S., 24
Washington, L. A., 141
Watzlawick, P., 143
Weakland, J., 10, 147
Wertheimer, M., 18-19
Whorf, B. L., 50
Wilkinson, L., 141-142
Williams, J. S., 30, 139
Witt, J. C., 140-141

Yager, G. G., 141

Zukav, G., 14

SUBJECT INDEX

Abduction, 12-13, 70-72
   systemic suggestions for, 72
Acausality, 66-69
   systemic suggestions for, 68-69
Ackerman Institute, 40, 48

Behavior setting, 26-28
Blame, 66-69, 75

Causality, 66-69
Change
   discontinuous, 16, 41-43, 77-79
      systemic suggestions for, 78-79
Circularity, 58-61
Community psychology, 25-32
Communication
   levels of, 11
   rules for, 40
Counterparadox, 39, 42

Deduction, 69
Double bind theory, 10-11
Dynamic models, 76-77
   systemic suggestions for, 77

Ecological psychology, 26-28
Epistemology, 16-17, 41, 43-45, 54-57
   systemic suggestions for, 56-57
Ethics, 99-101, 149-150

Field theory, 18, 24
Functional psychology, 18-21

Gestalt psychology, 18-19
Greek chorus, 47-48

Heisenberg Principle of Uncertainty, 55

Individualism, 146
Induction, 70

Language, 23, 50-54
   systemic suggestions for, 53-54
Linearity, 57-66
   systemic suggestions for, 64-66
Logic, 69-72

Mechanism, 8
Mental retardation, 29-30

Naive realism, 55
Newtonian world view, 6, 8
Nodal point, 36
Nonlinearity, 57-66

Patterns
   and rules, 73-76, 82
      systemic suggestions for 74-76
   which connect, 12-13, 79-80
Peabody College of Vanderbilt University, xiii
Philosophy,
   and science, 4-7
   Eastern, 5, 13-14
Positivism, 77-78
Public policy, 30-32

Quantum mechanics, 8, 13-14, 31

SUBJECT INDEX

Recursion, 57-66
  systemic suggestions for, 64-66
Reasoning
  forms of, 69-72
Recursive, 62-64
Relationship, 14, 19
Relevance, 80

Sense of community, 28-29
Stasis, 76-77
Stories, 11-12, 79-82, 109-110
  systemic suggestions, 82
Swampscott conference, 25
Systemic psychology, 3
  families and, 33-48
  schools and, 88-91, 102-135
    strategies for, 103-119
      establishing the focus group, 104-105
      positive connotation, 110-112
      prescriptions, 113-114
      recursive questioning, 108
      referral, 103-104
      ritual, 114-115
      storytelling, 109-110
      the team, 105-106
      working method, 106-107
  case simulation for, 120-135

goals for, 115-116
the future, 148-149
the referred person, 117-119
Systems psychology, 3-4
  in the schools, 136-144
    classroom environment approaches, 142-144
    ecosystemic approaches, 136-138
    related systemic approach, 142-144
    school psychology approaches, 140-141
    the liaison function, 138-140

Transaction, 20, 22-23
Transactional-ecological psychology, xiii

Unity, of observer and observed, 17, 55-57

Values, 30-32

Wholes, 72-73
  systemic suggestions for, 73
World views, 7-8
  Eastern, 7, 54
  Western, 8, 54

ABOUT THE AUTHOR

After working for several years as a master's level family counselor and school psychologist, Jeanne M. Plas received her Ph.D. in school psychology at the University of Georgia. Since 1975, she has been a member of the clinical, community, and school psychology doctoral training program at Peabody College of Vanderbilt University. She is the author of several book chapters and many journal articles covering a range of topics related to the theoretical and philosophical foundations of psychology and its applied practice. Her research interests have included the learning patterns of American Indian children and various family based variables that are implicated in weight disorders as well as family related factors that influence commitment to a physically fit lifestyle.